Collins

Collins Revision

GCSE Higher
Biology
Revision Guide

FOR OCR GATEWAY B

About this book

This book covers GCSE Biology for OCR Gateway B at Higher Level. Written by GCSE examiners, it is designed to help you to get the best grade in your GCSE Biology exams.

The book is divided into three parts; a topic-by-topic revision guide, workbook practice pages for each topic and detachable answers.

How to Use It

The revision guide section gives you complete coverage of each of the six modules that you need to study. Use it to build your knowledge and understanding.

The workbook section is packed with exam-style questions. Once you have covered each topic, use the matching workbook page to check your level.

The answers in the back of the book are detachable. Remove them to help to test yourself or a friend.

Go Up a Grade

There are lots of revision guides for you to choose from. This one is different because it really helps you to go up a grade.

Every topic in the revision guide and workbook sections is broken down and graded to show you what examiners look for at each level. This lets you check where you are, and see exactly what you need to do to improve your grade at every step. Crucially, it shows you what makes the difference between a C–D and an A–B grade answer.

Special Features

- **Questions** at the end of every topic page quickly test your level.
- **Top Tips** give you extra advice about what examiners really want.
- **Summaries** of each module remind you of the most important things to remember.
- **Checklists** for each module help you to monitor your progress.
- A comprehensive **glossary** gives you a quick reference guide to the Biology terms that you need to know.

Published by Collins
An imprint of HarperCollins*Publishers*
77–85 Fulham Palace Road
Hammersmith
London W6 8JB

Browse the complete Collins catalogue at
www.collinseducation.co.uk

© HarperCollins*Publishers* Limited 2010

10 9 8 7 6 5 4 3 2 1

ISBN-13 978 -000-734807-7

British Library Cataloguing in Publication Data
A Catalogue record for this publication is available from the British Library

Written by Louise Smiles
Series Consultant Chris Sherry
Project Manager Charis Evans
Design and layout Graham Brasnett
Editor Mitch Fitton
Illustrated by Kathy Baxendale, IFA design Ltd,
Mark Walker, Bob Lea and Steve Evans
Indexed by Marie Lorimer
Printed and bound in the UK by Martins the Printers,
Berwick Upon Tweed

Acknowledgements
The Authors and Publishers are grateful to the following for permission to reproduce photographs:

Science Photolibrary p11, p13/Photos.com p16, p17, p50, p65, p72, p75, p94/istockphoto p53, p58/ Geophotos p75/Mary Evans Picture Library p78/ Colin Bell p96/Tek Image p107.

Whilst every effort has been made to trace the copyright holders, in cases where this has been unsuccessful, or if any have inadvertently been overlooked, the Publishers will be pleased to make the necessary arrangements at the first opportunity.

Contents

Fit for life

Respiration

- Respiration that uses oxygen is called **aerobic respiration**.
  glucose + oxygen → carbon dioxide + water + energy

- During hard exercise not enough oxygen gets to the muscle cells. The cells also have to carry out **anaerobic respiration**. Less energy is released from anaerobic respiration.
  glucose → **lactic acid** + energy

- When lactic acid collects in muscles it causes pain and fatigue.

> **Top Tip!**
> Read the question carefully. It is easy to get confused between aerobic respiration and anaerobic respiration.

- The symbol equation for **aerobic respiration** is:
  $$C_6H_{12}O_6 + 6O_2 \rightarrow 6CO_2 + 6H_2O + energy$$

- During a sprint race, muscles cannot get oxygen quickly enough and an **oxygen debt** builds up. Muscle cells use anaerobic respiration to release some energy.

- The energy released during anaerobic respiration is less than that from aerobic respiration because glucose is only partly broken down.

- At the end of the sprint:
  – breathing rate stays high for a few minutes to replace the oxygen
  – heart rate stays high so blood can carry lactic acid to the liver where it is broken down.

Fitness

- After exercise, heart rate and breathing rate take time to return to normal. The fitter someone is, the faster they return to normal.

- However, fit people still become ill. Being fit does not stop infection by bacteria.

- Cardio-vascular efficiency, strength, stamina, agility, speed and flexibility are all ways of measuring fitness.

Blood pressure

- Blood pressure is measured in millimetres of mercury. This is written as **mmHg**.

- Blood pressure has two measurements:
  – **systolic pressure** is the maximum pressure the heart produces
  – **diastolic pressure** is the blood pressure between heart beats.

- Diet, exercise and age can affect blood pressure.

- People with high blood pressure are often asked to fill in a questionnaire about their lifestyle.

Blood pressure questionnaire

Questions	Notes	Answers Yes	No
1 Do you take regular exercise?	Strong heart muscles will lower blood pressure		✓
2 Do you eat a healthy balanced diet?	Reducing salt intake will lower blood pressure		✓
3 Are you overweight?	Being overweight by 5 kg raises blood pressure by 5 units	✓	
4 Do you regularly drink alcohol?	A high alcohol intake will damage liver and kidneys	✓	
5 Are you under stress?	Relaxation will lower blood pressure	✓	

What changes should this person make?

- Someone with **high blood pressure** would be at increased risk from small blood vessels bursting, brain damage, strokes and kidney damage.

- **Low blood pressure** can cause problems such as poor circulation, dizziness and fainting.

Questions

(Grades D–C)

1 Write down the word equation for anaerobic respiration.

(Grades B–A*)

2 Explain why someone breathes faster even after exercise stops.

3 Suggest what is meant by the term 'cardio-vascular efficiency'.

(Grades D–C)

4 What lifestyle factors can affect blood pressure?

What's for lunch?

Food

- Proteins from meat and fish are called **first class proteins**. They contain **amino acids** which can't be made by your body.

- In developing countries children often suffer from protein deficiency (**kwashiorkor**).

- To calculate the recommended daily amount (**RDA**) of protein, use the formula:
  RDA (in grams, g) = 0.75 × body mass (in kilograms, kg)

- A balanced diet depends on age, gender and activity.

- To calculate Body Mass Index (**BMI**) use this formula:
  $$BMI = \frac{mass\ (in\ kilograms,\ kg)}{height\ (in\ metres,\ m)^2}$$

- A BMI chart is used to see if you are the correct weight.

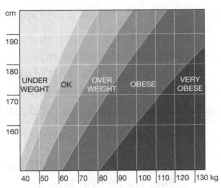

Look up your height and weight on the BMI bands to see where you come.

Diet

- Different people choose to have different diets for health or religious reasons.
  – Jews don't eat pork.
  – Some people have a nut allergy and mustn't eat nuts.
  – Vegetarians don't eat meat or fish and think it's wrong to kill and eat animals.
  – Vegans don't eat any foods of animal origin, including milk, cheese and eggs.
     They get their protein from cereals, beans, peas and nuts.

- Some people are influenced by the 'perfect' images they see in magazines. This often gives them a poor self-image and can lead to them having a poor diet.

- People with poor diets have increased health risks such as heart disease and diabetes.

Digestion

- Parts of the digestive system produce **enzymes** which break down carbohydrates, proteins and fats into smaller soluble molecules. These **diffuse** through the walls of the small intestine and into the blood plasma (carbohydrates and proteins) or lymph (fats) and pass to the cells.

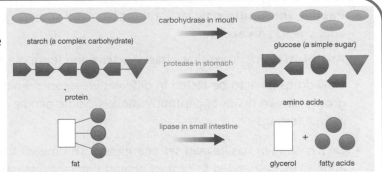

Examples of different enzymes.

- The stomach makes **hydrochloric acid** to help the enzyme called pepsin work.

- Fats are difficult to digest and absorb because they are not soluble in water.

- To help with fat digestion the gall bladder produces **bile** which **emulsifies** fats. This increases their **surface area** for enzymes to act on.

Questions

Grades D-C

1 Calculate the RDA for someone with a body mass of 80 kg.

Grades B-A*

2 Suggest why magazines can give some people a poor self-image.

Grades D-C

3 What do digestive enzymes do?

Grades B-A*

4 Explain how emulsification of fats is different to digestion of fats.

Keeping healthy

Microorganisms and disease

- Mosquitoes are called **vectors** and carry microorganisms that cause malaria. Malaria is caused by a protozoan that is a **parasite** as it gets its food from its living **host**, humans. Mosquitoes pass malaria on when they bite humans.

> **Top Tip!**
> Mosquitoes carry pathogens that cause diseases; they don't carry diseases.

- Lifestyle and diet can cause different disorders.
  - A diet high in sugar often causes **diabetes**.
  - Not enough vitamin C causes **scurvy**.
  - People develop **anaemia** if they don't eat enough iron.
  - Eating a healthy diet and not smoking can reduce the risk of developing some cancers.

- Some disorders are inherited. For example, genes cause red-green colour deficiency.

- Knowledge of a vector's **life cycle** is useful in preventing the spread of disease. The mosquito larva (young stage) lives in water. Draining stagnant water kills them. Spraying **insecticide** can kill the adult mosquito. A drug called Larium can be taken by people to kill the protozoan in their blood.

- Cancer is a result of cells dividing out of control. The new cells may form tumours.
  - **Benign** tumour cells, such as in warts, are slow to divide and harmless.
  - **Malignant** tumours are cancer cells, which divide out of control and spread around the body.

Protection against microorganisms

- Symptoms of a disease are caused by the pathogen damaging cells or making **toxins**.

- Pathogens have **antigens** on their surface. When a pathogen invades the body, white blood cells make **antibodies**, which lock on to the antigens and destroy the pathogen.

- **Active immunity** happens when a pathogen invades the body a second time. The white blood cells recognise it and make antibodies quickly destroying the pathogen before the symptoms occur. Active immunity can last a lifetime.

- **Passive immunity** only lasts a short time and you are given antibodies in a **vaccine**.

- **Antibiotics** are drugs that attack bacteria and fungi but not viruses.

- New drugs have to be tested in different ways: on animals, specially grown human tissue or computer models. Some people object to animal testing.

- Each pathogen has its own set of antigens. This means that specific antibodies are needed to protect against different diseases.

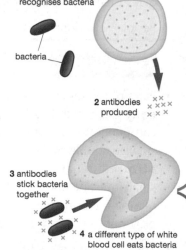

1 this white blood cell recognises bacteria

bacteria

2 antibodies produced

3 antibodies stick bacteria together

4 a different type of white blood cell eats bacteria

How white blood cells work.

- Excessive use of antibiotics has lead to an increase in resistant forms of bacteria. An example is the 'superbug' MRSA.

- To test a new drug, doctors use groups of volunteers. Some take the drug and some take a harmless pill called a **placebo**. In some trials the volunteers don't know which treatment they are receiving (**blind trial**). In other trials the doctors also don't know which treatment is used (**double blind trial**); other doctors keep this information.

Questions

Grades D-C
1 Explain why mosquitoes are called vectors.

Grades B-A*
2 Describe the difference between benign and malignant tumours.

Grades D-C
3 Describe the role of antibodies.

Grades B-A*
4 Describe the difference between blind and double blind drugs trials.

Keeping in touch

Eyes

- **Binocular vision** helps us to judge distances because the range of vision from two eyes overlaps. However, it only gives a small range of vision compared to monocular vision.

- People are short- or long-sighted because their eyeballs or lenses are the wrong shape.

- About ten per cent of the population experiences problems with colour vision. Some people lack specialised cells in their retinas. This causes red-green colour deficiency, which is inherited.

- The eye focuses light by changing the size of the lens. This is called **accommodation**.

- To focus on **distant** objects, the ciliary muscles relax and tighten the suspensory ligaments. This pulls the lens, making it thin.

- To focus on **near** objects, the ciliary muscles contract, the suspensory ligaments slacken and the lens becomes fat. The fatter the lens the more it refracts the light.

- As we get older the muscles become less flexible and it becomes harder to focus.

- Glasses or contact lenses can be used to correct some eye problems.

- Cornea surgery can also correct vision. Lasers are used to change the shape of the cornea.

Top Tip!
Use diagrams to help your revision. Exam questions on eyes often ask you to label a diagram.

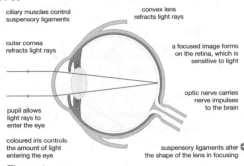

ciliary muscles control suspensory ligaments

convex lens refracts light rays

outer cornea refracts light rays

a focused image forms on the retina, which is sensitive to light

optic nerve carries nerve impulses to the brain

pupil allows light rays to enter the eye

coloured iris controls the amount of light entering the eye

suspensory ligaments alter the shape of the lens in focusing

The parts of the eye.

a Short sight
◄—Eyeball too long—►

light rays from a distant object   concave lens corrects refraction of light rays so the image lands on the retina

b Long sight
◄—Eyeball too short—►

light rays from a distant object   convex lens corrects refraction of light rays so the image lands on the retina

Concave and convex lenses correct short and long sight.

Top Tip!
A **concave** lens curves inwards like a 'cave'. A **convex** lens curves outwards.

Neurones

- **Motor neurones** carry impulses to the **muscle**.

- The nerve impulse is carried in the **axon** of the neurone.

- A **reflex arc** shows the direction in which an impulse travels: stimulus → receptor → sensory neurone → central nervous system → motor neurone → effector → response.

- Touching a hot plate results in a **spinal reflex arc**.

- Neurones are adapted to quickly carry and pass on nerve impulses.
  – They can be very long (nearly 2 metres).
  – They have branched endings (**dendrites**) to pick up impulses.
  – They are insulated by a fatty sheath, so that the electrical impulses don't cross over.

- Signals travel from one neurone to another across a gap called the **synapse**.

branching dendrites

muscle fibres (effector)

cell body   axon

nucleus   sheath

A motor neurone.

electrical impulse travels down the first neurone

axon

synapse

impulse triggers release of acetylcholine which diffuses across synapse

cell body of second neurone

new impulse generated in the second neurone

How a signal travels.

Questions

1 Name the part of the eye that controls the amount of light entering it.

2 Explain why it is harder to focus as we get older.

3 Write the following in the correct order so that they describe a reflex arc.

**effector   CNS   motor neurone   sensory neurone
receptor   stimulus   response**

4 Suggest why an impulse can only travel one way across a synapse.

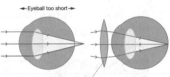

Drugs and you

Drugs

- Drugs are classified by law based on how dangerous they are and the penalties for possession.

	class A	class B	class C
maximum prison sentence	7 years and fine for possession	5 years and fine for possession	2 years and fine for possession
types of drugs	heroin, methadone, cocaine, ecstasy, LSD, magic mushrooms	amphetamines, barbiturates	anabolic steroids, Valium®, cannabis

- Here are some examples of different drugs:
  - depressants: alcohol, solvents and temazepam
  - hallucinogens: cannabis and LSD
  - painkillers: aspirin and heroin
  - performance enhancers: anabolic steroids
  - stimulants: ecstasy and caffeine.

- Different people have different views on drugs. Some people in the UK believe that the personal use of drugs, such as cannabis, should be allowed. They argue that prohibition of alcohol in America in the 1930s didn't stop its use; it simply created organised crime. Other people highlight scientific studies that show how dangerous and destructive these drugs can be.

- Nicotine acts as a **stimulant**. It affects synapses (see page 7). It stimulates the acetylcholine receptors allowing more impulses to pass.

- Alcohol is a **depressant**. It affects the brain, interfering with co-ordination and balance. It binds with acetylcholine receptors, blocking nerve impulses.

Tobacco

- Cells that line the trachea and bronchioles are called **epithelial cells**. Some cells have tiny hairs called **cilia** and others make sticky mucus.

- Cigarette smoke stops the cilia from moving and dust and particulates collect and irritate the cells. Smokers cough to move this mess upwards so it can be swallowed.

- Tars collect in air sacs and alveoli deep inside the lungs. They irritate the delicate lung tissue and are **carcinogens**.

- The tiny particulates in smoke also collect in lung tissue. They block the exchange of gases and reduce the amount of oxygen available to the rest of the body.

stops red blood cells getting oxygen

carbon monoxide

nicotine is addictive

irritates, causes cancer

tar

particulates

collect in lungs and block them

The effects of smoking on the body.

Top Tip!

In the exam you will need to interpret data on alcohol and cigarette smoke. Practice questions will help you with this skill.

Alcohol

Top Tip!

You need to be able to interpret information on reaction times, accident statistics and alcohol levels.

- The liver breaks down toxic chemicals such as alcohol. The liver can't deal with large quantities of alcohol. The alcohol kills the liver cells and causes **cirrhosis**.

- The alcohol content of a drink is measured in **units** of alcohol.

Questions

(Grades D-C)

1 Name a class A drug that is also a hallucinogen.

(Grades B-A*)

2 Describe the effect of a stimulant on the nervous system.

(Grades D-C)

3 Describe the effect of cigarette smoke on ciliated epithelial cells.

(Grades B-A*)

4 Describe the effect of particulates on the lungs.

Staying in balance

Homeostasis

D–C

- Various body systems keep the levels of oxygen, water, carbon dioxide and temperature constant. Keeping a constant internal enviroment is called **homeostasis**.

- Sweat comes from **sweat glands** in the skin and needs heat energy to evaporate. It takes heat from the body, cooling it down.
  - If your body gets too hot you could suffer from heat stroke or **dehydration**.
  - If your body gets too cold you could suffer from **hypothermia**.
  - If your body continues to get too hot or too cold you could die.

B–A*

- The temperature of the body is controlled by a feedback mechanism. It is called a **negative feedback** since sweating negates (cancels out) the increasing temperature.

- The body is kept at 37 °C because it is the **optimum temperature** for enzymes.

- The **hypothalamus** is a gland in the brain which detects the temperature of the blood. If blood temperature changes, the hypothalamus triggers protective measures such as changing the size of blood capillaries in the skin (**vasoconstriction** and **vasodilation**).

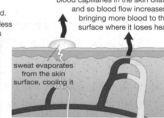

Vasoconstriction and vasodilation.

Vasoconstriction. When the body is too cold. blood capillaries in the skin constrict and so less blood flows through them, reducing heat loss

Vasodilation. When the body is too hot. blood capillaries in the skin dilate and so blood flow increases, bringing more blood to the surface where it loses heat

sweat evaporates from the skin surface, cooling it

Hormones and diabetes

D–C

- Some people have **diabetes** because their **pancreas** doesn't make enough **insulin**.

- Diabetes can be controlled by eating a diet low in sugar or by an injection of insulin. Insulin lowers the level of glucose in the blood.

- The size of the insulin dose a diabetic needs depends on their diet and exercise.

B–A*

- When levels of glucose in the blood are too high, insulin converts some glucose into glycogen, which is stored in the liver.

Sex hormones

D–C

- Ovaries start producing **sex hormones** when girls reach **puberty**. The hormones cause breasts to develop and hips to widen. Hair starts to grow in the pubic area and under armpits. Periods start because the ovaries have begun to release an egg every month.

- **Testes** produce male sex hormones. Boys become more muscular, grow facial hair and their voice breaks. Their testes start to produce sperm and genitals develop.

- All these developments are called **secondary sexual characteristics**.

- **Oestrogen** and **progesterone** control the **menstrual cycle**. Oestrogen causes the repair of the uterus wall and progesterone maintains it. Together they control **ovulation**.

B–A*

- Synthetic hormones can be used in contraception; they stop ovulation (egg release) by mimicking pregnancy. Female sex hormones are also used to treat infertility such as lack of eggs.

Questions

Grades D-C

1 Explain what is meant by the term 'hypothermia'.

Grades B-A*

2 Explain what is meant by the term 'vasodilation'.

Grades D-C

3 Describe one secondary sexual characteristic of girls and boys.

Grades B-A*

4 Describe the role of sex hormones in the menstrual cycle.

Gene control

Genes

D–C

- The **genetic code** is in a chemical called DNA (**deoxyribonucleic acid**). Sections of DNA form a gene.

- In DNA the two strands look like a twisted ladder. The shape is called a **double helix**.

- The rungs of the ladder are made of **four** different chemicals called **bases**. The specific arrangement of bases makes up the unique genetic code (or recipe) that makes you.

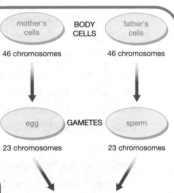
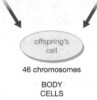

DNA.   The bases in DNA.

Cells

How the chromosome number is made.

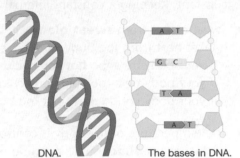

D–C

- The number of **chromosomes** in a cell is usually an even number. This is because the paired chromosomes separate when eggs and sperm are formed.

- Different species have different numbers of chromosomes in each of their body cells. The camel has 70; the squirrel has 40; the mosquito has 6; and humans have 46.

- Eggs and sperm (**gametes**) have only one chromosome from each pair (23 in total). They combine to make a fertilised egg that has 46 chromosomes.

Top Tip!

Make sure you write a clearly explained answer to a question. Always read your answer through. If it doesn't make sense to you, it won't make sense to the examiner!

- Your body is made up of one hundred million million cells (100 000 000 000 000)!

B–A*

- Each cell has a complete set of instructions contained in the DNA of its chromosomes. Even a cell in your big toe has information about your eye colour. Since this information isn't needed in your big toe cells, these genes are **switched off**.

DNA

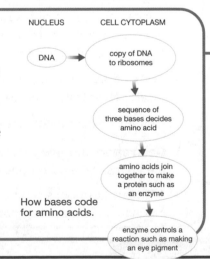

B–A*

- The four bases in DNA are shown by their initials **A**, **T**, **C** and **G**. **A** only links with **T** and **C** only links with **G**. This is important when DNA is copied because it only needs one side of the DNA ladder. The specific sequence of bases gives the genetic code.

- DNA contains codes for the production of specific **enzymes**. These in turn control cell reactions that produce specific chemicals, such as coloured eye pigments. Therefore DNA controls whether you have blue, brown or green eyes.

How bases code for amino acids.

Questions

Grades D-C

1 How many different bases are there in a chromosome?
2 How many chromosomes are there in the sperm cell of a camel?

Grades B-A*

3 Which base joins with base A in DNA?
4 Explain how DNA controls eye colour.

Who am I?

Male or female?

D–C

- All humans have 46 chromosomes, arranged in pairs, in their body cells.

- One pair of chromosomes is the **sex chromosome**:
  – females have an identical pair, **XX**
  – males have a non-indentical pair, **XY**.

B–A*

- Each sperm carries either an X or a Y sex chromosome and has a random chance of fertilising an egg.

- There is an on-going debate over the balance between genetic (**nurture**) and environmental (**nature**) factors in determining human attributes, such as intelligence, sporting ability and health. Are great athletes made or were they born with the right genes?

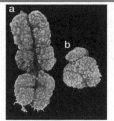

a X and **b** Y sex chromosomes magnified highly. How is the shape of the X chromosome different from that of the Y chromosome?

There should be equal numbers of males and females in the human population.

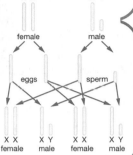

Characteristics

D–C

- Humans are all different; they show **variation**. Variation is caused by genes being mixed up in gametes, fertilisation and changes in genes or chromosomes called **mutations**.

- Mutations change the DNA base sequence, stopping the cell making the protein the gene is normally coded for. They can be caused by radiation, chemicals or can occur spontaneously.

- Some mutations are harmful, such as haemophilia, while others can be advantageous.

Inheritance

D–C

- Some characteristics are **dominant** over others and more people will show the dominant characteristic than the **recessive** one. For example, lobed ears are dominant over ears with no lobes.

- **Breeding experiments** can be carried out to find dominant characteristics. The offspring (F₁ generation) of this cross all show the dominant purple colour.

B–A*

- A **monohybrid cross** involves only one pair of characteristics. These are carried on a pair of chromosomes; one chromosome carrying the dominant **allele**, the other chromosome carrying the recessive allele. Alleles are different versions of the same gene. The dominant allele will always show up if the individual is **heterozygous**.

- This diagram shows how symbols are used to work out the **genetic cross** for cystic fibrosis.

- Cystic fibrosis is an inherited condition caused by a recessive gene. When both healthy parents are heterozygous for the condition (they are Cc) there is a one in four chance of their baby being **homozygous** (cc) for cystic fibrosis. Carriers of cystic fibrosis have to make important decisions, such as should they risk having children with cystic fibrosis?

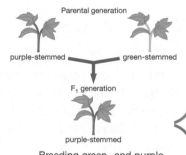

Breeding green- and purple-stemmed tomato plants.

A genetic diagram for cystic fibrosis.

Questions

Grades B-A*

1 Identical twins can be used to research the debate on nature verses nurture. Suggest a reason why.

Grades D-C

2 Name one cause of a mutation.

Grades D-C

3 More people have brown eyes than blue. Which colour is recessive?

Grades B-A*

4 Draw a genetic diagram to show how cystic fibrosis is inherited from healthy parents.

B1 Summary

Diet and exercise

The **Body Mass Index** (BMI) can be used to indicate being under or over weight.

Digested food is absorbed.

Enzymes chemically digest food.

Fatigue is linked to oxygen debt.

Anaerobic respiration releases less energy than aerobic respiration.

Our energy comes from **aerobic respiration** or **anaerobic respiration**.

High blood pressure can damage the brain and kidneys.

Blood pressure has two readings:
– **diastolic** pressure
– **systolic** pressure.

A **balanced diet** contains food such as:
– **carbohydrates**
– **proteins**
– **fats**
– **nutrients** such as **minerals** and **vitamins**.

Hormones, sense organs and reflexes

Insulin controls the blood sugar level.

Endocrine glands produce hormones such as **insulin** and **sex hormones**.

Reflexes are fast reactions that do not involve the brain.

Oestrogen and **progesterone** control the **menstrual cycle**.

Neurones carry **electrical impulses**.

The body temperature of 37 °C is linked to the **optimum temperature** for enzymes.

Feedback mechanisms help to maintain a constant internal environment.

Drugs and disease

Tobacco and alcohol are called '**social drugs**'. Tobacco smoke contains many chemicals such as nicotine and tar. Alcohol affects judgement and causes liver and brain damage.

Harmful drugs are classified as class A, B and C. Any class A drug such as cocaine is dangerous and addictive.

New drugs must be tested in trials.

The mosquito is a **vector** that carries malaria.

Fungi, bacteria, viruses and protozoa can cause disease. They are **pathogens**.

Infectious diseases are easily passed on.

Our **immune system** and **immunisation** protect against infections.

Genes

Genes control the production of proteins such as enzymes.

The **coded information** is the sequence of bases in DNA.

Cystic fibrosis, red-green colour deficiency and sickle cell anaemia are inherited genetic disorders

Inherited disorders are caused by **faulty genes**.

We have **23 pairs** of **chromosomes**.

Some human characteristics are **inherited** and some are caused by the **environment**.

The **genetic code** is coded information in genes which make up chromosomes.

Ecology in our school grounds

Ecosystems

D–C

- We know more about the surface of the Moon than we know about the deepest ecosystems of our oceans.

- Animals from the deep can't live near the surface and are rarely seen. For example, the giant squid can grow up to 20 m long but suffocates in warm surface water. To see it in its natural habitat requires very expensive submarines. A human would be crushed due to the increased pressure at such depths.

The giant squid.

- Many new species may exist at depths that humans can't reach.

B–A*

- Oceans are natural ecosystems; they exist without any help from humans.

- There are many artificial ecosystems controlled by humans. A field of wheat is mainly artificial. Farmers try to control what grows and lives there.
  - They use **herbicides** to remove weeds.
  - They use **pesticides** to control pests.
  - They can increase the crop yield by adding **fertilisers**.

- **Biodiversity** describes the range of living things in an ecosystem. The farmer decreases the biodiversity of his farm when he uses herbicides and pesticides.

Counting animals

D–C

- To estimate a **population**, scientists can use a method called 'mark and recapture'.
  - The animals are trapped and marked in some harmless way.
  - They are then released and the traps are set again a few days later.

- To estimate the population the following formula is used.

$$\frac{\text{number of animals caught first time} \times \text{number of animals caught second time}}{\text{number of marked animals caught second time}} = \text{population}$$

- Population sizes will always be changing because:
  - animals are being born and others are dying
  - there is movement of animals in and out of the ecosystem.

> **Top Tip!**
>
> A **population** is a group of animals or plants of the same species. A **community** is lots of different species living in the same ecosystem.

B–A*

- To estimate a plant population, scientists can use **quadrats**.
  - The quadrat is put on the ground and the percentage cover of each plant is recorded.
  - The quadrat is placed in a random way to ensure a fair representation of an area.

- To increase the accuracy of an estimate:
  - the process is repeated several times
  - the sample size is as large as possible.

- Scientists have to remember that their samples may be unrepresentative of the population as a whole.

Questions

(Grades D-C)

1 What happens to a giant squid in warm surface water?

(Grades B-A*)

2 Name the type of chemical used to remove
a weeds **b** pests.

(Grades D-C)

3 What is meant by the term 'population'?

(Grades B-A*)

4 Describe one method used to place quadrats in a random way.

Grouping organisms

Plants and animals

- Vertebrate animal groups have different characteristics.
  - **Fish** have wet scales and gills to get oxygen from the water.
  - **Amphibians** have a moist permeable skin.
  - **Reptiles** have dry scaly skin.
  - **Birds** all have feathers and beaks, but not all of them can fly.
  - **Mammals** have fur and produce milk.

Top Tip!

You may be asked about a vertebrate you have never heard of. Don't worry, it will fit into one of the five groups

- This table shows the main differences between plants and animals.

	food	shape	movement
plants	make their own food using chloroplasts to trap energy from the Sun	spread out to collect plenty of water and nutrients from soil	stay in one place, they cannot get up and move somewhere else
animals	cannot make their own food, so they need to eat	more compact than plants to help them move around	able to move around to find food

Odd ones out

- Some organisms don't fit into the animal kingdom or the plant kingdom.
  - Mushrooms cannot move like an animal or make food like a plant. They belong in the kingdom called **fungi**.
  - *Euglena* can make their own food or they can feed. They belong in the kingdom called **protoctista**.
  - *Archaeopteryx* has bird and reptile characteristics. It is thought to represent the evolutionary link between reptiles and birds.

- Dolphins and whales are special animals. They are mammals, yet they have **evolved** to look like fish so they can live in water.

- **Hybrids** are the result of breeding two animals from different species, such as the donkey and the horse to produce a mule. Hybrids are sterile and can't breed. It's not a species and therefore it's difficult to classify.

What is a species?

- A tiger and a lion are both cats. However, they are two different **species**.

- Members of the same species can breed. Lions breed with other lions to make young lions. These young lions will be **fertile**.

- All cats belong to the same **family**. The family is called Felidae. Each species of cat is given its own scientific name. Lions have the name *Panthera leo*. Tigers are called *Panthera tigris*. They both have the same first name because they are closely related.

- The lion and the tiger share a recent ancestor but have evolved to live in different **habitats**. Lions live in open grassland while tigers prefer forest.

- Cheetahs and leopards aren't closely related. However, they are very similar because they are **adapted** to the same habitat.

Questions

Grades D-C

1 Explain why plants need chloroplasts.

Grades B-A*

2 Explain why mushrooms are not classified as plants.

3 Explain why dolphins need to look like fish.

Grades D-C

4 What is the family name for cats?

The food factory

Photosynthesis

D–C

- Photosynthesis can be described using this word equation:

carbon dioxide + water $\xrightarrow[\text{(chlorophyll)}]{\text{(light energy)}}$ glucose + oxygen

- The products of photosynthesis are **glucose** and **oxygen**.

- Glucose is transported as **soluble** sugars to parts of the plant where it is needed.

- The glucose can be used by the plant in these ways:

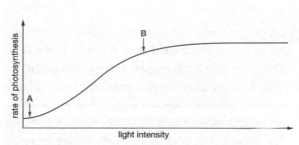

used to make cellulose for plant cell walls

used as energy

stored as starch

used to make proteins for plant growth

stored as fats and oils

photosynthesis → glucose

oxygen

used in respiration   released into air

How the products of photosynthesis are used.

B–A*

- The overall balanced chemical equation for photosynthesis is:

$$6CO_2 + 6H_2O \xrightarrow[\text{(chlorophyll)}]{\text{(light energy)}} C_6H_{12}O_6 + 6O_2$$

- For storage, the glucose joins together to make larger molecules of starch. Starch is:
  – insoluble and therefore not easily lost from the cell in solution
  – not very reactive, making it a good storage molecule.

Increasing and limiting photosynthesis

D–C

- The following actions increase the rate of photosynthesis:
  – keeping plants warm   – increasing the amount of light.
  – giving plants extra carbon dioxide

B–A*

- This graph shows the effect of light intensity on the rate of photosynthesis:
  – the rate of photosynthesis increases as the light intensity increases until point B
  – at point B, the rate of photosynthesis stays the same, something else is limiting it
  – the limiting factor could be carbon dioxide level or temperature
  – carbon dioxide, light intensity and temperature are all **limiting factors** of photosynthesis.

Why does the curve in the graph flatten out?

rate of photosynthesis

B

A

light intensity

Respiration and gas exchange

D–C

- **Respiration** uses oxygen to release energy from glucose. At the same time it releases carbon dioxide and water.

B–A*

- As long as a plant is photosynthesising it needs to take in carbon dioxide. At the same time it will release oxygen.

- At night the plant still needs oxygen for respiration. It takes in oxygen from the air and releases carbon dioxide.

Top Tip!

Plants carry out respiration 24 hours a day, not just at night. If they stopped respiring they would have no energy and would die.

Questions

Grades D-C
1 Name three uses of glucose in a plant.

Grades B-A*
2 Write out the balanced equation for photosynthesis.

Grades D-C
3 Name three actions that increase the rate of photosynthesis.

Grades B-A*
4 Explain why plants give out carbon dioxide at night.

Compete or die

Plant and animal competition

- Bluebells flower in spring to catch as much light as possible before the leaves are fully out on the trees, causing shade. In summer the bluebells find it difficult to grow as the larger trees take most of the light, water and minerals. The bluebells and trees are in **competition** with each other.

- Animals often compete to attract a mate so that they can breed. Animals need to breed so that the species survives. Male elephant seals fight each other in order to keep their mates.

> **Top Tip!**
>
> If you're asked about animals or plants you have never heard of, don't be put off.
> All animals and plants compete for similar things.

- All organisms have a role to play in an ecosystem. For example, the role of a squirrel is to live in woods and eat acorns. This role is called the squirrel's **ecological niche**. In Britain, there are two types of squirrel: the red squirrel and the American grey squirrel. At one time they both occupied the same niche, but in different countries. Now they compete for the same niche in Britain. The grey squirrel is 'outcompeting' the red squirrel.

Animal relationships

- There are many ways in which animals of different species interact.
  - Lions eat antelopes. If there are lots of lions, antelope numbers will go down as more get eaten. When there are fewer antelopes, lion numbers go down as there is not enough food.
  - The tapeworm is a **parasite**. It lives in the digestive system of other animals including humans. The tapeworm takes food away from its **host** so that it can grow.
  - The sharksucker is a fish that attaches itself to sharks. It cleans the shark's skin by eating its parasites. In return, the shark protects the sharksucker from predators. Relationships like this where both animals benefit is called **mutualism**.

- Some species are totally dependent on others. The pea plant is a **legume**. It has structures on its roots called **root nodules**. Bacteria live inside the nodules and convert nitrogen into nitrates. They are called **nitrogen-fixing bacteria**. The bacteria give the pea plant extra nitrates to help it grow and the pea plant gives the bacteria sugar which they turn into energy.

Populations and cyclic fluctuation

- Predator–prey relationships play an important part in controlling populations.

- The 'up and down' pattern of population change is called **cyclic fluctuation**.
  This graph shows the cyclic fluctuation of the snowy owl population and its prey, the lemming.

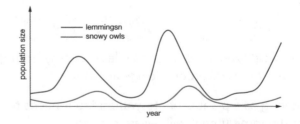

Why are the peaks in the snowy owl population slightly behind the peaks in the lemming population?

Questions

1 Explain why animals need to compete for a mate and breed.

2 The red squirrel population of Britain has gone down. Suggest a reason.

3 What is meant by the term 'mutualism'?

4 Explain why the snowy owl population rises when the lemming population rises.

Adapt to fit

Animals and adaptation

D–C

- Camels live in the **desert**. They are well adapted to survive the heat and lack of water.
  - All their body fat is in the hump, so heat can be lost from the rest of the body.
  - Stored fat in the hump can be used when there is no other food available.
  - Their body temperature can rise above normal, so they don't need to sweat.
  - Bushy eyelashes and hair-lined nostrils stop sand getting in.
  - Large feet spread out their weight to stop them sinking into the sand.

- Polar bears live in the **Arctic**. They are well adapted to the cold.
  - They have thick white fur for camouflage and insulation.
  - A layer of fat over its body called **blubber** keeps it insulated.
  - A large body compared to its surface area stops it losing too much heat.
  - Small ears reduce the surface area from which heat can be lost.
  - Sharp claws and teeth help it to seize and eat prey.
  - Strong legs aid running and swimming.
  - Large feet spread its weight on the snow.
  - Fur-covered soles on its paws help them grip and insulate them from the cold.

- Brown bears and polar bears live in different habitats. Brown bears would find it difficult to exist in the polar bear's habitat because they aren't adapted for the cold.

> **Top Tip!**
>
> Make sure you know the different meanings of 'describe' and 'explain'.
> - The camel has large feet – is to 'describe' an adaptation.
> - The camel has large feet to spread the load on sand – is to 'explain' an adaptation.

Plants and adaptation

B–A*

- **Cacti** are plants that live in the desert. They are well adapted to hot dry conditions.
  - They have long roots to reach as much water as possible.
  - A thick waterproof **cuticle** reduces water loss.
  - A fleshy stem stores water.
  - Leaves have become spines to reduce water loss and to stop animals getting at the water in the stem.
  - Photosynthesis takes place in the green stem.
  - Round shape reduces the plant's **surface area**, cutting down water loss.

- The cactus is adapted to the desert and wouldn't survive in Britain as there's too much water which would cause it to rot.

- In order to reproduce, plants need to transfer pollen from one plant to another. The process they use is called **pollination**. Plants have adapted to carry out pollination in two ways.
  - Wind pollinated plants have feathery stigmas and small, light pollen.
  - Animal pollinated plants have colourful petals, nectar and 'sticky' pollen.

Questions

Grades D-C

1 Explain why camels have bushy eyelashes.
2 Describe how polar bear feet are adapted to life in the Arctic.

Grades B-A*

3 Explain why a cactus needs a thick cuticle.
4 Suggest a reason why some plants make nectar.

Survival of the fittest

Fossils

- Fossils form in different ways.
  - Hard parts such as shells and bones can be replaced by minerals, which turn to stone.
  - Some organisms sink into mud and then **casts** or **impressions** form when they decay.
  - Organisms can be preserved in **amber**, peat bogs, tar pits or ice.

- The **fossil record** shows how organisms have changed. Not all living things have a complete fossil record, because:
  – some body parts decay quickly before they can be fossilised
  – fossilisation is rare and most living things will completely decay
  – there may still be fossils we have not found.

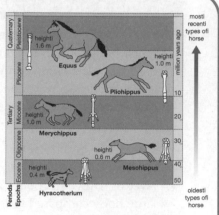

How the shape of the horse's foot has evolved over time.

Interpretation of the fossil record

- Some scientists use the fossil record to show how animals and plants have evolved. Other scientists have used the gaps in the fossil record to argue against evolution.

- Many complex organisms in the fossil record appear and then disappear which **Creationists** interpret to mean that organisms were created and did not evolve.

Natural selection

- Environments can change. To survive these changes a species needs to adapt and evolve otherwise it will become **extinct**. In any species, it's only the best adapted that survive.

- This **survival of the fittest** is called **natural selection**. **Genes** pass on the successful characteristics of a species to the next generation. These are examples occurring today.
  - Peppered moths are dark or pale in colour. Dark moths are better camouflaged in polluted areas, so more of them survive.
  - Rats have evolved to become resistant to the poison warfarin.
  - Bacteria are becoming resistant to antibiotics.

Evolution

- Charles **Darwin** developed the theory of natural selection.
  - Within any species there is **variation**.
  - There will be competition for limited resources such as food.
  - Only those best adapted will survive, called survival of the fittest.
  - Successful adaptations are passed to the next generation in genes.
  - Over time, the changes may result in a new species.
  - The less well adapted species may become extinct.

- Jean Baptiste de **Lamarck** had a different theory called the law of **acquired characteristics**. His theory was discredited because acquired characteristics cannot be passed on by genes.

Top Tip!

You need to be able to use natural selection to explain how bacteria have become resistant. Remember, it's all about survival of the fittest and passing on genes.

Questions

Grades D-C

1 Write down one reason why the fossil record is incomplete.

Grades B-A*

2 Explain how Creationists interpret gaps in the fossil record.

Grades D-C

3 How do rats pass on resistance to warfarin to the next generation?

Grades B-A*

4 Write down the main points in Darwin's theory of evolution.

Population out of control?

Pollution

D–C

- Increasing levels of carbon dioxide cause **climate change** and sulphur dioxide causes **acid rain**.

- An increase in the use of chemicals called CFCs has led to a depletion of the ozone layer.

Top Tip!

Try not to mix up the three main effects of pollution. It's CFCs that deplete the ozone layer, *not* carbon dioxide.

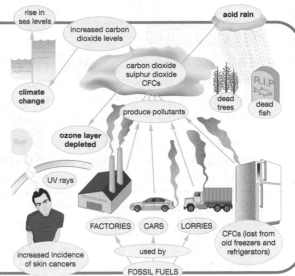

The main effects of pollution.

Population and pollution

B–A*

- The graph shows the past, present and predicted future world human population.

- The human population is growing at an ever-increasing rate. This is called **exponential growth**.

- The increasing population is quickly using up the Earth's resources and increasing pollution.

- The world population figures show the greatest rise in population is occurring in under-developed countries such as Africa and India.

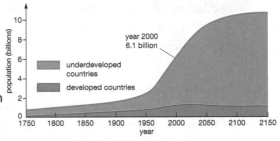

A graph showing exponential growth.

- However, if the countries that use the most fossil fuels are considered, developed countries such as the United States of America and Europe seem to be causing the problem.

- America is the heaviest user of oil, using about 50 L per person each day.

Indicator species

D–C

- The presence or absence of an **indicator species** is used to estimate levels of pollution.
  - The stonefly larva is an insect that can only live in clean water.
  - The bloodworm, water louse, sludge worm and rat-tailed maggot are animals that can live in polluted water.
  - Lichen grows on trees and rocks but only when the air is clean. It is unusual to find lichen growing in cities. This is because it is killed by the pollution from cars.

Top Tip!

You only need to remember that indicator species are used. You don't have to remember the level of pollution that each species tolerates.

B–A*

- Animals have different sensitivities to environmental conditions. In rivers and ponds, different animals can tolerate different pollution levels.
  - The sludge worm lives in polluted water because it can cope with very low oxygen levels.
  - The alderfly cannot live in polluted water. It cannot tolerate low oxygen levels.

- Water that contains lots of different species (higher biodiversity) is usually a healthy environment.

Questions

Grades D-C

1 Which gas causes acid rain?

Grades B-A*

2 Explain why the USA causes more pollution than Ethiopia.

Grades D-C

3 Name two indicator species that can live in polluted water?

Grades B-A*

4 Explain why the alderfly cannot live in polluted water.

Sustainability

Extinction

- Animals become **endangered** or **extinct** because:
  - their climate changes and they cannot adapt fast enough
  - their habitat is destroyed or becomes polluted
  - they are hunted by humans or outcompeted by better adapted animals.

- Animals can be saved from extinction by:
  - protecting habitats or setting up **artificial ecosystems** and **captive breeding** in zoos
  - making hunting illegal and educating people about the reasons to save them.

D–C

Conservation

- Conservation programmes such as saving the rainforest are important because:
  - they protect plants and animals that could be used for food or medicine
  - protecting species low down in the food chain helps those higher up to survive
  - resulting tourism can benefit local communities, helping them to maintain their culture.

B–A*

Whales

Whale parts have many uses.

- Live whales are important as people can make money from the tourist trade.

- Some whales are kept in captivity for research, breeding programmes or entertainment. Many people object when whales lose their freedom.

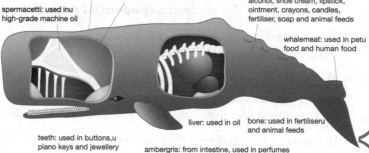

skin: used in belts, shoes,u handbags and luggage

spermacetti: used inu high-grade machine oil

sinews: used in tennis rackets

oil: sperm whale oil taken from bone and skin used in high-grade alcohol, shoe cream, lipstick, ointment, crayons, candles, fertiliser, soap and animal feeds

whalemeat: used in petu food and human food

liver: used in oil

bone: used in fertiliseru and animal feeds

teeth: used in buttons,u piano keys and jewellery

ambergris: from intestine, used in perfumes

D–C

- Some countries want to lift the ban on whaling. Scientists need to kill some whales to find out how they survive at extreme depths. Migration patterns and whale communication can only be investigated if the animal is alive.

B–A*

Sustainable development

- **Sustainable development** is a way of taking things from the environment but leaving enough behind to ensure a supply for the future and to prevent permanent damage.
  - Fishermen have been set **quotas** so that there are enough fish left to breed.
  - People are educated about the importance of maintaining species' numbers for future generations.
  - Woods are re-planted to keep up the supply of trees.

D–C

- As the world population increases, it is even more important to carry out sustainable development on species such as whales.

- The demand for food and other resources could lead to an increase in whaling. The whaling nations will need to work together to prevent extinction.

- When whaling quotas are set, other factors will need to be taken into account such as pollution levels and over-fishing of the whales' food.

B–A*

Questions

(Grades D-C)

1 Explain why 'climate change' could lead to extinction of some species.

(Grades B-A*)

2 Suggest a reason how tourism could help maintain local culture.

(Grades D-C)

3 Suggest a reason why people object to keeping whales in captivity?

4 Suggest one way Britain could help sustain the rainforest in Brazil.

B2 Summary

Ecosystems

Different counting methods are used to estimate populations.
These estimates are often inaccurate if the sample size is not large enough.

All the living things and their surroundings make up an ecosystem.

Keys can be used to identify the animals and plants in a habitat.

Artificial ecosystems are often controlled using pesticides, herbicides and fertilisers.

Many ecosystems are still unexplored and could contain new species.

Classification

The **animal kingdom** is split into two groups:
– **vertebrates**
– **invertebrates**.

There are five vertebrate groups:
– **fish**
– **amphibians**
– **reptiles**
– **birds**
– **mammals**.

Plants can make their own food by a process called photosynthesis:

$$\text{carbon dioxide} + \text{water} \xrightarrow[\text{(chlorophyll)}]{\text{(light energy)}} \text{glucose} + \text{oxygen}$$

$$6CO_2 + 6H_2O \xrightarrow[\text{(chlorophyll)}]{\text{(light energy)}} C_6H_{12}O_6 + 6O_2$$

Competition and survival

Whales could still be hunted to extinction. Their population needs to be sustained.

Animals and plants adapt to their **habitats**. Those better adapted are more able to **compete** for resources. Species that cannot adapt may become **extinct**. **Fossils** provide evidence of extinct species.

The **survival** of a species depends on how well it can adapt to changes in the environment.
The number of predators can affect population numbers of prey and vice versa.
Survival may also depend on the presence of another organism:
– **mutualism**
– **parasitism**.

Indicator species are used to monitor pollution levels.

The population of predators and prey regulate themselves, this is called **cyclic fluctuation**.

The increase in human population is leading to an increase in pollution and loss of habitat. As habitats become smaller species are unable to compete and become extinct.
Species can be protected from extinction if resources are carefully managed – **sustainable development**.

Molecules of life

Cells

- **Cell respiration** is carried out inside **mitochondria**. During respiration, energy is released from glucose in the presence of oxygen.

DNA

- The structure of DNA helps it to copy itself every time a cell divides. This is called **DNA replication**.

- DNA is split into sections called **genes**. Each gene holds the code for making a protein that our bodies need by using amino acids from our food. Proteins are made by joining amino acids into a chain. The DNA controls the order of amino acids and the production of proteins is called **protein synthesis**.

- DNA can be used to identify people by **DNA fingerprinting**, which produces a pattern of unique bands like a barcode:
  - blood or cell sample is isolated
  - DNA is extracted
  - restriction enzymes are used to fragment the DNA
  - DNA fragments are placed on gel
  - fragments are separated by an electric curent (electrophoresis)
  - banding of DNA fingerprint can be matched.

- The order of bases found in DNA is called the base code. Each three bases code for an amino acid. Cells use these base codes to join amino acids together in the correct order.

- Amino acids can be changed in the liver into any that are missing from the diet.

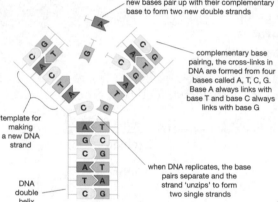

DNA replication. The double strand 'unzips' and two new double strands are formed.

new bases pair up with their complementary base to form two new double strands

complementary base pairing, the cross-links in DNA are formed from four bases called A, T, C, G. Base A always links with base T and base C always links with base G

template for making a new DNA strand

when DNA replicates, the base pairs separate and the strand 'unzips' to form two single strands

DNA double helix

Enzymes

- An **enzyme** is a biological **catalyst**; it's a protein that speeds up a biological reaction. Enzymes catalyse most chemical reactions occurring within cells such as respiration, photosynthesis and protein synthesis. Each enzyme is **specific** to a **substrate**. In an enzyme-catalysed reaction, substrate molecules are changed into **product** molecules.

- Each enzyme has a unique sequence of amino acids so each enzyme has a different shape. Within this shape is an **active site**. Once the substrate is attached to the active site it is turned into a **product**. The enzyme is like a lock and the substrate like a key. Enzymes are **denatured** when the shape of the active site changes.

- Enzymes have an **optimum pH** when the active site and the substrate molecule are a perfect fit. Changing the pH denatures the enzyme.

- As the temperature increases, the molecules gain more energy. More collisions occur and the rate of reaction increases. Above the optimum temperature, the enzyme denatures and the reaction stops. Lowering the temperature again will have no effect, as the enzyme shape can't be changed back.

Questions

1 Describe how proteins are made.

2 How many bases code for one amino acid?

3 What is meant by the term 'enzyme'?

4 Explain why high temperature stops an enzyme joining to a substrate.

Diffusion

Grades

D–C

B–A*

D–C

B–A*

D–C

B–A*

Diffusion

- **Diffusion** is the movement of a substance from an area of high concentration to an area of low concentration.

- **Molecules** move **randomly** in all directions, but most will move from an area of high concentration. Therefore **diffusion** is the net movement of particles from an area of high **concentration** to an area of low concentration due to the random movement of individual particles.

- The **rate of diffusion** can be increased by: increasing the **surface area**, decreasing the diffusion distance or a greater concentration difference.

Diffusion in humans

- **Alveoli** in the **lungs** have a higher concentration of oxygen than the blood that surrounds them, so the oxygen diffuses into the blood. Carbon dioxide diffuses from the blood into the alveoli. To maintain this **gas exchange**, breathing takes place.

- After **eating** there is a high concentration of digested food molecules in the small intestine, which causes them to diffuse through the cells of the small intestine wall into the blood.

- A **foetus** needs to be supplied with food and oxygen from its mother so that it can develop. The mother's blood and the foetus's blood come close together in the **placenta**. Dissolved food and oxygen pass into the foetus's blood and carbon dioxide and waste products pass out into the mother's blood by **diffusion**.

- Villi in the small intestine and alveoli in the lungs have special adaptations to increase the rate of diffusion.

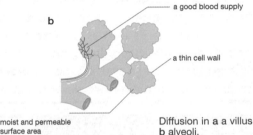

a — a thin wall for easy diffusion of food into the blood — a good blood supply — long, permeable villi to increase surface area — moist and permeable surface area

b — a good blood supply — a thin cell wall

Diffusion in **a** a villus **b** alveoli.

- To speed up movement across the **placenta**, it has a **huge surface area** with a thin wall so substances only have a short distance to diffuse.

- A **synapse** is a gap between two neurones (nerve cells). To carry a signal from one neurone to the next, the synapse releases a transmitter substance which can diffuse across the gap between the two neurones.

Diffusion in plants

- Carbon dioxide diffuses into the leaf through small pores called stomata. During photosynthesis, oxygen levels increase inside the leaf, which causes oxygen to diffuse out of the leaf. **Water** is lost by **diffusion** and **evaporation**.

- To increase the rate of **gas exchange**, the leaf has a **large surface area** with lots of **stomata** on the under-surface.

Questions

(Grades D-C)

1 What is diffusion?

(Grades B-A*)

2 Explain why villi are important for food absorption.

3 Describe the function of a transmitter substance.

(Grades D-C)

4 Describe how oxygen is lost from the leaf.

Keep it moving

Blood cells

- **Red blood cells** are adapted to carry as much oxygen as possible. They contain **haemoglobin**, which joins to oxygen, and have **no nucleus** so there's more room to store oxygen. They are **disc-shaped** and have a **dent** on both sides to help absorb oxygen. They are **tiny** so they can carry oxygen to all parts of the body.

- **White blood cells** change shape so they can wrap around (**engulf**) microbes. They don't fight or kill microbes.

- Food, water, hormones, antibodies and waste products are carried in the **plasma**.

- The shape of a red blood cell means it has a large surface area compared to its volume. This enables it to absorb a lot of oxygen.

- In the lungs **haemoglobin** reacts with **oxygen** to form **oxyhaemoglobin**. When it reaches tissue it separates into haemoglobin and oxygen. The oxygen diffuses into the tissue cells and the red blood cells return to the lungs to pick up more oxygen.

D–C

B–A*

Heart

- The **valves** of the heart prevent backflow of blood.

- Coronary arteries supply the heart with **food** and **oxygen**.

- Too much cholesterol in the diet can cause serious **heart problems** and even the need for a **heart transplant**. There are some problems with heart transplants such as: shortage of donors, rejection, dependency on drugs, and difficulty in matching tissue to age and size. Using **mechanical replacements** also has problems, such as the size of the replacement, the power supply needed and the chance of rejection.

RIGHT — LEFT

pulmonary artery, takes deoxygenated blood to the lungs

aorta, takes oxygenated blood to the body

semi-lunar valve

vena cava, brings deoxygenated blood from the body

right atrium

tricuspid valve

valve tendon

right ventricle, thinner wall as pumps blood a relatively short distance to the lungs

pulmonary vein, brings oxygenated blood from the lungs

left atrium

bicuspid valve

left ventricle, has thick muscular wall to pump blood at higher pressure all the way round the body

The structure and function of the heart.

D–C

The circulatory system

- **Arteries** transport blood away from the heart. They have thick muscular and elastic walls to help them withstand high blood pressure as blood leaves the heart.

- **Veins** transport blood to the heart. They have a large lumen to help blood flow at low pressure; valves stop blood from flowing the wrong way.

- **Capillaries** join arteries to veins. They have a thin, permeable wall to allow exchange of materials such as oxygen between the capillaries and the body tissue.

- Humans have a **double circulatory system**. One circuit links the heart and lungs, and one circuit links the heart and the body. Blood going to the body can be pumped at a much **higher pressure** than blood going to the lungs. This provides a greater rate of flow to the body.

- Sometimes **cholesterol** in the blood sticks to the inside of artery walls. As it builds up, it forms a plaque that restricts the flow of blood. Some of this cholesterol can break away and block the artery completely.

D–C

B–A*

Questions

Grades D-C

1 Name the chemical in blood that joins to oxygen.
2 Name the blood vessel that takes blood to the lungs.
3 Explain why an artery needs a thick muscular wall.

Grades B-A*

4 What is the advantage of the double circulatory system?

Divide and rule

Multi-cellular

D–C

- Humans are made up of millions of cells: they are **multi-cellular**. This gives them many advantages.
  – Multi-cellular organisms can grow large.
  – Cell **differentiation** takes place. Cells change shape or size to carry out different jobs.
  – Organisms become more complex and develop different organ systems.

B–A*

- The size that a single cell can grow to is limited by its surface area to volume ratio.
  If the cell is too large it can't absorb enough food and oxygen through the surface of its membrane to stay alive. This is why large multi-cellular organisms have developed transport systems.

Mitosis

D–C

- Humans have **23 pairs** of **chromosomes**. The chromosomes in a pair look the same and carry similar information. They are called **homologous** pairs. When a cell has pairs of chromosomes it's called a **diploid** cell (i.e. it has the full set of chromosomes).

- During growth, a type of cell division called **mitosis** makes new cells. The new cells are exact copies and contain 23 pairs of chromosomes.

B–A*

- Mitosis makes **genetically identical** cells.

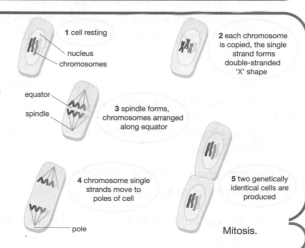

1 cell resting
nucleus
chromosomes

2 each chromosome is copied, the single strand forms double-stranded 'X' shape

equator
spindle

3 spindle forms, chromosomes arranged along equator

4 chromosome single strands move to poles of cell

pole

5 two genetically identical cells are produced

Mitosis.

Meiosis

D–C

- Gametes have half a set of chromosomes called the **haploid number**. During fertilisation the gametes join to form a **zygote**. The zygote is diploid and can develop into an embryo.

- **Meiosis** is a special type of cell division that produces gametes. Reproduction using meiosis results in a lot of genetic **variation** within a species.

B–A*

- Gametes are made when diploid cells divide by meiosis to produce haploid cells. Meiosis involves two divisions: first the pairs of chromosomes separate, then the chromosomes divide in the same way as in mitosis.

pole

1 homologous chromosomes pair up

2 one from each pair moves to opposite poles

3 strands of chromosomes move to opposite poles

4 four new haploid cells form

Meiosis.

Moving sperm

D–C

- **Sperm** are specially adapted to swim a long way. Each sperm has lots of **mitochondria** to release energy for motion. **Acrosome** on the sperm head releases enzymes that digest the cell membrane of an egg allowing the sperm inside.

Questions

Grades B-A*

1 Explain why the size of a cell is limited by its surface area to volume ratio.

Grades D-C

2 How many chromosomes are there in a diploid human cell?

Grades D-C

3 Name the type of cell division that produces haploid cells.

Grades B-A*

4 Describe one way in which meiosis and mitosis are the same.

Growing up

Cells

D–C

- This table shows how plant and animal cells are similar and different.

plant cell	animal cell
has nucleus, cytoplasm and cell membrane	has nucleus, cytoplasm and cell membrane
cellulose cell wall for support	no cell wall
most have chloroplasts for photosynthesis	no chloroplasts
large vacuole containing cell sap	may have a small vacuole but no cell sap

- A few days after an egg is fertilised it contains a group of cells called **stem cells** which all have the same simple cell structure. They divide and then differentiate to form all the different specialised cells in the body. As the embryo grows all the specialised cells form **tissues** and **organs**.

- Scientists have found ways of making stem cells develop into other specialised cells in the hope of replacing damaged cells. However, many people object to stem-cell research because it can involve human embryos. Scientists use embryos because they are easier to grow than adult stem cells.

B–A*

Growth

D–C

- Animals and plants grow in different ways. Animals tend to grow to a certain size and then stop. Plants can continue to grow.

- The cells of animals and plants cause them to grow in different ways.

B–A*

plant	animal
most growth is due to cells elongating (growing longer), not dividing	growth is due to cells dividing
cell division only normally occurs at the tips of shoots and roots	cell division occurs all over the body
many cells never lose the ability to differentiate	most animal cells lose the ability to differentiate very early on

Gestation

D–C

- **Gestation** is the length of time from fertilisation to birth. The larger the animal the longer gestation tends to be. This is because the animal needs time to develop enough to survive outside the uterus. An elephant has a gestation of 700 days but a rat only has 22 days.

- Different parts of the **foetus** and **baby** grow at different rates. The brain and head develop quickly to co-ordinate the complex human structure and chemical activity.

- After a baby is born, it has regular growth checks. The baby's weight and head size are recorded to check that the baby is growing at a normal rate.

  – Poor weight gain can indicate problems with a baby's digestive system.
  – Larger than normal head size can indicate that fluid is collecting on the brain or that the separate skull bones are not fusing together.

B–A*

Questions

(Grades D-C)

1 Name two structures found in plant cells but *not* animal cells.

(Grades B-A*)

2 Explain why scientists use embryo stem cells instead of adult stem cells.

(Grades D-C)

3 Explain why elephants have a longer gestation period than mice.

(Grades B-A*)

4 Suggest a reason for poor weight gain in babies.

Controlling plant growth

Plant hormones

D–C

- Farmers, gardeners and fruit growers mostly use man-made **plant hormones** such as **synthetic auxin**. This is sprayed on selected crops to kill weeds and is known as a **selective weedkiller**.

- **Rooting powder** is used to stimulate roots to grow from plant cuttings.

- Hormones are used to make fruit grow without the flowers being fertilised. This means the fruits have no pips, such as seedless grapes.

- A hormone called **ethene** is sprayed on bananas to ripen them ready for sale.

- The seeds taken from a parent plant are **dormant**, which means germination won't take place. Hormones are used to break the dormancy and make the seed germinate.

Responses

D–C

- A plant is **sensitive** and responds to different **stimuli**.

- A hormone called **auxin** controls the response. This is made in the tips of roots and shoots and travels through a plant in **solution**.
  - Plant **shoots** grow **towards light** – **positive phototropism**.
  - Plant **roots** grow **away from light** – **negative phototropism**.
  - Plant **shoots** grow **away from** the pull of **gravity** – **negative geotropism**.
  - Plant **roots** grow **with** the pull of gravity – **positive geotropism**.

Top Tip!

The 'positive' and 'negative' terms are difficult to remember. If it's positive it grows towards the stimulus. Imagine being positively attracted to someone!

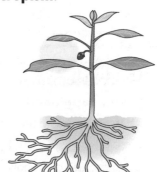

Shoots are positively phototropic and negatively geotropic.
Roots are negatively phototropic and positively geotropic.

How auxin works

B–A*

- When the tip of a shoot is cut off it stops growing because it removes the source of **auxin**. If the tip is replaced on the stem it starts to grow again.
  - Auxin is made in the tip.
  - Auxin moves away from light and collects on the shady side of a shoot.
  - Auxin causes cells on the shady side to **elongate** (grow longer) more than cells on the light side.
  - The shady side becomes longer and causes the shoot to bend.

light all around

untreated
seedling

substance **X**

treated
seedling

Can you explain why the shoot with substance X is bent?

seedlings at start → after 2 days

Questions

Grades D–C

1 Describe the effect of rooting powder on plant cuttings.
2 Which part of the plant shows positive geotropism?

Grades B–A*

3 Describe the effect auxin has on cells in the shoot.
4 Explain why auxin causes the shoot to bend towards the light.

New genes for old

Selective breeding

- **Selective breeding** is used to breed a cow that has a high yield of creamy milk.
  - Choose types of cows that produce lots of milk (Friesians) or creamy milk (Jerseys).
  - **Cross-breed** them by mating a cow with a bull.
  - Select the best offspring that produce large quantities of creamy milk.
  - Repeat the selection and breeding process for a number of generations.

- Selective breeding often involves animals that are closely related. This is called **inbreeding** and causes a reduction in the **gene pool** (the different genes available in a species). With a smaller gene pool there is less **variation** and the more chance there is of harmful recessive genes being expressed.

Mutation

- Changes to genes, called **mutations**, usually cause harm to the organism. For example, in **haemophilia** the blood doesn't clot.

- Some mutations can be advantageous and give a better chance of survival, such as bacteria that can mutate and become resistant to antibiotics.

- Mutations can be caused by radiation (X-rays), chemicals in cigarette smoke or by chance.

- When a gene mutates the DNA **base sequence** is changed, which alters the protein or even prevents its production.

Genetic engineering

- **Genetic engineering** involves adding a gene to the DNA of an organism. For example, a bacterium has been genetically engineered to make human insulin for people with diabetes.

- Rice doesn't contain vitamin A. Scientists have taken the gene to make **beta-carotene** from carrots and put it into rice plants. Humans eating this rice can then convert the beta-carotene into vitamin A.

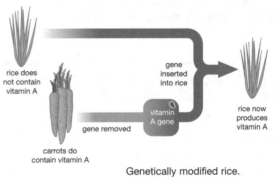

Genetically modified rice.

- Scientists are developing crops that are resistant to herbicides, frost and disease. This will enable more crops to grow in difficult places but the gene may have harmful effects on humans who eat the plants.

- Modifying DNA by genetic engineering follows the following basic steps:
  - select the **characteristic**
  - identify and **isolate** the gene
  - **insert** the gene into the chromosome of a different organism
  - **replicate** (copy) the gene in the organism and produce the protein.

Top Tip!

You must be able to debate the issues involved with GM organisms.

Questions

Grades D-C

1 Describe the main processes in selective breeding.

Grades B-A*

2 Describe the effect of inbreeding on animals.

Grades D-C

3 Suggest one disadvantage of genetically modified crops.

Grades B-A*

4 List the basic steps in genetic engineering.

More of the same

Cloning animals

- **Embryo transplantation** can be used to clone cows. Embryo calves are placed in surrogate mothers to develop in the normal way.

- **Human embryos** could also be cloned to provide **stem cells**. These could be transplanted into people suffering from diabetes so that they could make their own insulin. However, people are concerned that this would be unethical because the embryo is a living thing. Some people are also afraid that scientists will clone adult humans.

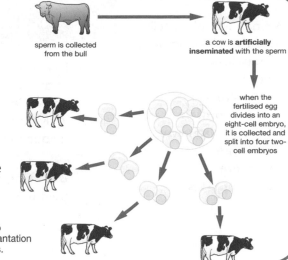

sperm is collected from the bull

a cow is **artificially inseminated** with the sperm

when the fertilised egg divides into an eight-cell embryo, it is collected and split into four two-cell embryos

Embryo transplantation in cows.

each embryo is then **implanted** into a surrogate cow where it grows into a calf. All the calves will be genetically identical to each other, but not to their parents

egg cell taken from sheep A and nucleus removed

cells taken from the udder of sheep B and the nucleus removed

nucleus from sheep B is put into egg of sheep A

egg cell is put into a female sheep to grow

Dolly the sheep was cloned using a process called **nuclear transfer**.

cell grows into a clone of sheep B

- There are considerable **risks** involved in cloning:
  - there is a low rate of success
  - research into human cloning raises many moral and ethical issues
  - Dolly died of conditions linked to old age, yet she was only seven years old.

- But there are also some **benefits** of cloning:
  - cloned pigs could make up for a shortage in transplant organs
  - diseases could be cured using embryonic stem cells.

Cloning plants

- Here are some **advantages** of cloning plants:
  - cloning produces lots of identical plants more quickly
  - cloning enables growers to produce plants that are difficult to grow from seed.

- And some **disadvantages**:
  - the plants are all genetically identical so if the environment changes or a new disease breaks out, it's unlikely that any of the plants will survive
  - cloning plants over many years has resulted in little genetic variation.

- Small sections of plant tissue can be cloned using **tissue culture**. This must be carried out using **aseptic technique** (everything has to be sterile).
  - Plants with the desired **characteristics** are chosen.
  - A large number of small pieces of **tissue** are taken from the parent plant.
  - They are put into sterile test tubes that contain **growth medium**.
  - The tissue pieces are left in **suitable conditions** to grow into plants.

- Plants are easier to clone than animals. Many plant cells retain the ability to **differentiate** into different cells but most animal cells don't.

Questions

(Grades D-C)

1 Name the process used to clone cows.

(Grades B-A*)

2 Name the process used to clone Dolly the sheep.

(Grades D-C)

3 Suggest one disadvantage of cloning plants.

(Grades B-A*)

4 Describe the stages involved in tissue culture.

B3 Summary

Molecules of life

Chromosomes are made of **DNA**. A section of DNA is called a **gene**. Each gene codes for a particular **protein**.

Animals and plant cells have the following parts:
– **membrane**
– **nucleus**
– **cytoplasm**
– **mitochondria**.
Plant cells also have:
– **cell wall**
– **vacuole**
– **chloroplasts**.

DNA is found in the **nucleus** of the cell. DNA carries **coded information**; individuals have their own unique DNA.

DNA fingerprints can be used to identify individuals.

Enzymes are **biological catalysts**, they catalyse chemical reactions in the body.

Proteins are made up of chains of **amino acids**. When the cell makes a new protein it has to join the amino acids together in the correct order. The base sequence in DNA determines the order of amino acids in the protein.

Blood and diffusion

Carbon dioxide and **oxygen diffuse** in and out of plants through the leaves.

Diffusion of substances takes place in the **placenta**. Food and oxygen diffuses into the foetal blood. Carbon dioxide and waste diffuses into the mother's blood.

Blood is moved around the body in:
– **arteries**
– **veins**
– **capillaries**.
The heart pumps the blood to the lungs and body.

In the lungs **oxygen** diffuses into **red blood cells**. **Carbon dioxide** diffuses from the blood into the **lungs**.

Food diffuses from the **small intestine** into the **blood**. The **alveoli** are adapted to increase the rate of diffusion.

Cell division and growth

There are five stages in human growth:
– **infancy**
– **childhood**
– **adolescence**
– **maturity**
– **old age**.

Eggs and sperm are special cells called **gametes**. A type of cell division called **meiosis** produces them. Gametes contain the **haploid** number of chromosomes. **Fertilisation** takes place when an egg and sperm join. The result is a diploid cell called a **zygote**.

Cells divide by **mitosis** so that organisms can grow and replace old cells.

After cells divide they become specialised. This is called **differentiation**. Undifferentiated cells are called **stem cells**. Stem cells can develop into different types of cells, tissues and organs.

Plant hormones

Plant **hormones** have commercial uses such as weedkillers and rooting powder.

The hormone called **auxin** is involved in the plant's response to light (**phototropism**) and the plant's response to gravity (**geotropism**).

Using cells and DNA

Selective breeding involves breeding organisms with the best characteristics.

Cloning involves producing genetically identical copies.

Genetic engineering involves taking **genes** from one organism and putting them into another.

Who planted that there?

The structure of a leaf

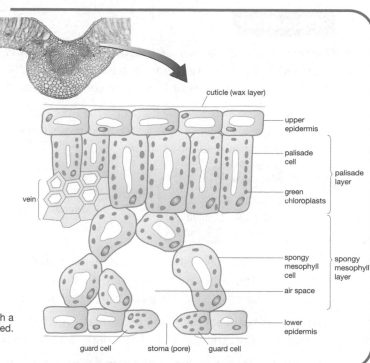

- When you cut through a leaf and look at it under a microscope you'll see many different cells.

- A **palisade** cell contains many **chloroplasts**. Photosynthesis occurs at a high rate in these cells and lots of sugars and starch are produced.

cuticle (wax layer)

upper epidermis

palisade cell

palisade layer

vein

green chloroplasts

spongy mesophyll cell

spongy mesophyll layer

air space

A stained section through a green leaf, magnified.

lower epidermis

guard cell   stoma (pore)   guard cell

Gas exchange in a leaf

- **Carbon dioxide** enters and **oxygen** exits a leaf through the **stomata** (one pore is called a stoma). The gases move by **diffusion**.

Photosynthesis

- The structure and arrangement of **cells** are adapted for maximum efficiency of **photosynthesis**.
  - The **epidermis** is thin and transparent, allowing light through to inner cells.
  - The **palisade** cells contain large numbers of chloroplasts to absorb lots of light energy.
  - The **chloroplasts** are arranged mainly down the sides of the palisade cells, allowing some light to reach the **mesophyll cells**.
  - **Air spaces** between mesophyll cells allow gases to diffuse easily and reach all cells.
  - The mesophyll cells are small and irregular. This increases their surface area to volume ratio so large amounts of gases can enter and exit.

- A **leaf** is adapted for photosynthesis by:
  - being **broad** so it has a large **surface area** to absorb light
  - being **thin** so gases don't have far to travel and light can reach all the way through it
  - having **chlorophyll** in most of its cells
  - having a **network** of specialised **cells in veins** to support it and carry water and sugars to different parts of the plant
  - having **stomata** to allow **gas exchange**: carbon dioxide to **diffuse** into it and oxygen to diffuse out of it.

Questions

(Grades D–C)

1 Which type of leaf cell contains the most chloroplasts?

(Grades B–A*)

2 Explain why there are air spaces between mesophyll cells.

(Grades D–C)

3 Explain why a plant leaf is broad.

4 What is the purpose of stomata?

Water, water everywhere

Osmosis

- **Osmosis** is the **diffusion of water** across a **partially permeable membrane** from an area of high water concentration to an area of low water concentration.

- Water will move into cells by osmosis when they are placed in water. Cells will lose water by osmosis if they are placed in strong sugar solution.

Top Tip!

Remember osmosis is about **water movement** not about salt or sugar molecules moving.

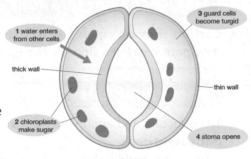

Osmosis in a plant cell.

- Potato chips placed in salt water become **flaccid** (soft and floppy). This is because there's a higher concentration of water molecules inside the potato cells than outside.

- When water **leaves** a plant cell by osmosis, the cell contents **shrink** and there's **less** water **pressure** against the cell wall. The cell contents are **plasmolysed** and the cell collapses.

- When water **enters** a plant cell it **swells up** and there's an **increase** in water pressure against the cell wall. This **turgor pressure** causes the cell to become **turgid** (hard and rigid).

- A **leaf** is adapted for **photosynthesis** so water easily evaporates and escapes from it. Plants need to reduce their water loss by having **few stomata**, which are mainly in the **lower epidermis**. Plants can also open and close their stomata.

- If a blood cell of an **animal** is placed in salt water or pure water it loses or gains water by osmosis. Since it has no cell wall for support it shrinks (becomes **crenate**) or bursts (**lysis**).

How a stomata opens.

Transpiration

- **Root hairs** are long and thin and have a large **surface area** to absorb lots of water from the soil by osmosis.

- The evaporation of water from leaves is called **transpiration**. It's useful because:
  - evaporation of water **cools** a plant
  - it brings **water** to the leaves for **photosynthesis**
  - a cell full of water gives **support**
  - the water moving up the stem carries useful **dissolved minerals**.

- To prevent too much water evaporating from the leaf it has a **waxy** covering called the **cuticle**, and **stomata** mainly on its shaded underside.

- The inelastic cell walls of a plant also help to support it.

Questions

(Grades D-C)

1 What name is given to the movement of water in and out of cells?

(Grades B-A*)

2 Describe the change you would see using a microscope if onion cells were placed in a strong salt solution.

3 Explain how osmosis is used to close the guard cell.

(Grades D-C)

4 Explain why stomata are mainly found on the underside of the leaf.

Transport in plants

Transport in plants

- **Xylem** and **phloem** are specialised cells that form the **transport system** in a plant. They form continuous **vascular bundles** from the roots to the stems and leaves.

- **Xylem cells** carry **water** and **minerals from the roots** to the leaves for photosynthesis. Some water evaporates and escapes by **transpiration** from the leaves.

- **Phloem cells** carry dissolved **food** such as **sugars from the leaves** to other parts of the plant. This movement is called **translocation**. The sugars can be used for growth or stored as starch.

Top Tip!

It's easy to get confused between xylem and phloem cells. Remember, phloem carries food.

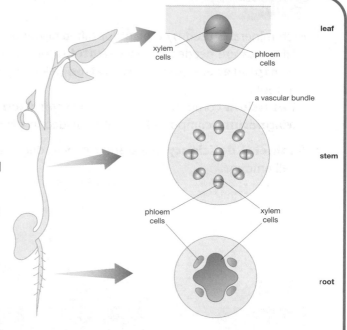

broad bean plant   sections

Horizontal cross-sections through a broad bean plant to show the arrangement of xylem and phloem.

- **Xylem cells** have thick, strong cell walls that contain a chemical called **lignin**.

- The **xylem vessels** are made of dead xylem cells joined to form a long hollow tube. The hole in the middle is called the **lumen**.

- **Phloem cells** also make long thin columns but the cells are still alive.

Increasing transpiration

- A **high rate** of **transpiration** happens when:
  - light intensity increases
  - temperature increases
  - air movement (wind) increases
  - humidity (amount of water in the atmosphere) falls.

- When **light intensity** increases, the stomata open allowing more water to escape.

- As the **temperature** increases, the random movement of water molecules increases and more water escapes.

- **Wind** causes more water molecules near stomata to be removed. This increases evaporation and diffusion of water from inside the leaf.

- In **dry conditions** there's a very low concentration of water molecules outside the leaf. This causes more diffusion of water from inside the leaf to the outside.

Questions

(Grades D-C)

1 Name the vessels that carry water and minerals up the stem.

(Grades B-A*)

2 Explain why xylem vessels are strong enough to support a tree.

(Grades D-C)

3 Name two things that increase the rate of transpiration.

(Grades B-A*)

4 Explain how increased light intensity increases transpiration rate.

Plants need minerals too

Minerals

- Each mineral is used by a plant for different things.
  - **Nitrates** are needed to make **proteins** for growth.
  - **Phosphates** are used in **respiration** (releasing energy) and are needed for growth, especially in roots.
  - **Potassium** compounds are used in **respiration** and in **photosynthesis**.
  - **Magnesium** compounds are also needed in **photosynthesis**.

- A **mineral deficiency** in a plant is easy to detect and correct. A mineral is needed only in a very small amount.

no nitrates ⟶ • poor growth
• yellow leaves

no phosphate ⟶ • poor root growth
• discoloured leaves

no potassium ⟶ • poor fruits and flowers
• discoloured leaves

no magnesium ⟶ • yellow leaves

   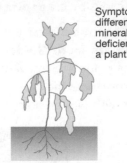

Symptoms of different mineral deficiencies in a plant.

- This is what happens to the minerals the plant takes in through fertilisers.
  - **Nitrogen** in nitrates is used to make **amino acids**. Amino acids are joined together to make different proteins such as **enzymes**.
  - **Phosphorus** in phosphates is used to make **cell membranes** and **DNA**. DNA carries genetic information.
  - **Potassium** is used to help make some enzymes. Enzymes speed up chemical reactions such as **photosynthesis** and **respiration**.
  - **Magnesium** is used to make **chlorophyll** molecules.

Active transport

- An increase in the uptake of minerals by a plant is matched by an increase in its **respiration rate**. This shows that **energy** is necessary for the uptake of minerals. The minerals are absorbed against a **concentration gradient**.

- A plant absorbs different minerals in different amounts and **selects** the minerals it needs.

- Special **carrier** molecules take the **mineral ions** across plant cell membranes by a process called **active transport**. Different carriers take different minerals.

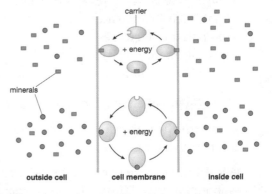

carrier

+ energy

minerals

+ energy

outside cell   cell membrane   inside cell

Active transport in a plant.

Top Tip!

Active transport needs energy from respiration but osmosis and diffusion don't.

Questions

Grades D-C

1 Name two minerals needed for photosynthesis.

2 Which mineral would you give a plant with poor root growth?

Grades B-A*

3 Which mineral is used to make chlorophyll?

4 Describe two differences between diffusion and active transport.

Energy flow

Food pyramids

- The links in food chains and food webs show different **trophic levels**. Energy is passed from one organism to another and each organism is at a different trophic level.

- The numbers of organisms at different trophic levels can be counted and the information shown in a **pyramid of numbers**.

- An animal that eats plants is called a **herbivore** and an animal that eats other animals is a **carnivore**.

- A **pyramid of biomass** is a better way of showing trophic levels because the mass of the organisms is used.

- As energy flows along a food chain some is used up in growth. At each trophic level about 90% of the energy is transferred into other less useful forms, such as heat from respiration and egestion of waste.

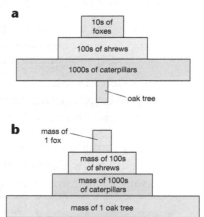

a a woodland food chain doesn't show a pyramid shape because only one large tree supports all the other organisms **b** a pyramid of biomass of the same food chain.

Biomass

- Because each trophic level 'loses' up to 90% of the available energy, the length of a food chain is limited to a small number of links.

- The shape of a **pyramid of biomass** shows that the energy decreases with increasing trophic levels.

- **Biomass** can be eaten; fed to other livestock (an inefficient transfer of energy); used as a source of seeds for next year (doesn't directly supply energy but saves costs); or used as a biofuel.

- To calculate the **efficiency of energy transfer** use this formula:

$$\text{efficiency} = \frac{\text{energy used for growth (output)}}{\text{energy supplied (input)}}$$

If there's 3056 kJ of energy in grass and only 125 kJ is used for a cow's growth:

$$\text{efficiency} = \frac{125}{3056} = 0.04 \text{ or } 4\%$$

This shows that the energy transfer to humans from beef is very inefficient.

Biofuels

- The energy from **biomass** can be used as **alternatives** to fossil fuels.
  - Fast-growing trees such as **willow** can be burnt in power stations. Because they are fast growing there's always a good supply.
  - Brazil produces a lot of **sugar cane** which is fermented using yeast to make alcohol. The process uses anaerobic respiration. The alcohol is mixed with petrol to make 'Gasohol', a fuel for cars.

- Here are some advantages of biofuels.
  - They're **renewable** by growing more plants or collecting methane.
  - They contribute less to air pollution.
  - Biofuels help towards a country's energy self-reliance.

Questions

(Grades D-C)

1 Describe the difference between a pyramid of numbers and a pyramid of biomass.

(Grades B-A*)

2 Calculate the efficiency if there's 2000 kJ of energy in grass and 40 kJ is used for growth of a cow.

(Grades D-C)

3 Explain how sugar cane can be used to fuel a car.

(Grades B-A*)

4 Explain why biofuels are renewable energy sources.

Farming

Intensive farming

- **Intensive farming** produces as much food as possible in the space available. Although it's an efficient method, it raises **ethical issues** such as cruelty to animals, and **environmental concerns** as the pesticides can pollute the land.

- Pesticides can build up to lethal doses in the food chain.
  - Pesticides from farmland get into lakes (0.02 ppm).
  - Microscopic life absorbs small amounts of the pesticide (5 ppm).

  - Fish eat large amounts of microscopic life and the pesticides build up inside them (200 ppm).
  - Grebes eat fish and the pesticide builds up killing them.

- Intensive farming is extremely **efficient** as more energy is **usefully transferred**. This is because:
  - there are fewer weeds and pests in crops
  - less heat is lost from animals kept in sheds and their movement is restricted.

Hydroponics

- A **hydroponics system** can be used to grow lettuce and tomato plants. The system doesn't use soil, so there's less chance of disease or pests affecting the plants. The plant roots are specially treated in water that contains the required amounts of fertiliser and oxygen. The system is also useful in countries with poor soil or little water to irrigate fields.

- A hydroponics system has many **advantages**.
  - Mineral supply is controlled and unused minerals are recycled, reducing cost.
  - It's set up under cover so there's better control of external conditions and disease.

- But there are some **disadvantages** too.
  - Manufactured fertilisers must be bought and tall plants such as tomatoes need support.

Some methods of organic farming

- **Weeds** are removed to reduce competition for light and minerals.

- **Seeds** are sown at **different times** so crops are ready at different times.

- **Beans** are grown to put nitrogen back into the soil. They're called **nitrogen-fixing plants**.

- **Manure** and **compost** are used in place of artificial fertilisers.

- **Crop rotation** is used so the same crops don't grow in the same place each year.

- Other **animals** can be used to kill pests, such as ladybirds that eat aphids. This saves on the use of harmful chemicals, but is often very slow to work and takes animals out of a food chain.

- Organic farming is a good idea in countries that *aren't* short of food. Other countries that have a poor climate can't produce enough organic food so they do need artificial fertilisers.

- The type of farming practised is a balance between **cost** and **suitability**.
  - In many developed countries it's fashionable to want organic food since it's seen to be healthier and people can afford to pay more.
  - In less well developed countries the farmers try to grow enough food, by any means possible, to survive.

Questions

Grades D-C

1 Suggest one way in which intensive farming is cruel to animals.

Grades B-A*

2 Suggest one advantage of hydroponics.

Grades D-C

3 Write down one way organic farmers can replace nitrogen lost from soil.

Grades B-A*

4 Suggest one disadvantage of organic farming.

Decay

Decay

- The remains of dead and decaying plants and animals are called **detritus**.

- Animals such as earthworms, maggots and woodlice depend on detritus for their food and are called **detritivores**.
  – Detritivores break down detritus into small pieces, which increases the surface area and so speeds up decay.
  – Detritivores are important as they **recycle** chemicals from dead plants and animals.

- Another method of using decay is for **compost**. These are the ideal conditions for speeding up the composting process:
  – **warmth**, by placing a compost bin in a sunny place
  – **moisture**
  – good **aeration**, such as regular mixing of the contents to allow oxygen in.

dead animal → blowflies and blowfly maggots → common frog → grass snake

decaying leaves → earthworms → blackbird → sparrowhawk

Two food chains to show how dead animals and decaying plant material are recycled.

- As **microorganisms** living in a compost bin **respire**, heat is transferred which warms up the compost, which in turn speeds up decay.

- Decay depends on **enzyme action**, so conditions that speed up enzyme action also speed up decay. The **optimum temperature** (the temperature at which enzymes work best) is approximately 37 °C for bacteria and 25 °C for fungi.

- **Aerobic** bacteria break down dead detritus quickly. They need a good supply of oxygen to carry out aerobic respiration.

- In a lack of oxygen, **anaerobic** bacteria grow. These produce acid conditions that slow down decay.

- A fungus that feeds off dead and decaying material is called a **saprophyte**. Its digestive enzymes are released on to the food and break it down into simple soluble substances so the digested food is absorbed.

Preserving foods

- **Canning** involves heating food to kill bacteria, then sealing the food in a can to stop bacteria getting in.

- **Cooking** kills bacteria. Food poisoning can be caused by food being undercooked.

- **Vinegar** is an acid. Very few bacteria can grow in acid conditions. Pickled eggs and chutney are preserved in this way.

- **Drying** foods, such as cereals, works because bacteria and fungi can't grow without water.

- **Freezing** kills bacteria or slows their growth; cooling just slows down the growth.

- **Adding sugar** or **salt** kills some bacteria and fungi and stops the growth of others.

Top Tip!

Remember any preserving method stops microbes growing because it takes away warmth, moisture or oxygen.

Questions

Grades D–C

1 Name three detritivores.

Grades B–A*

2 What is meant by the term 'optimum temperature'?

3 Explain what's meant by the term 'saprophyte'.

Grades D–C

4 Explain why drying prevents food decay.

Recycling

The carbon cycle

- **Carbon dioxide** is a compound that contains carbon.

- Carbon dioxide is **taken out** of the atmosphere by plants to use in **photosynthesis**. The carbon is then passed along the food chain when animals feed.

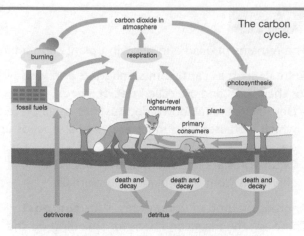

The carbon cycle.

- Carbon dioxide is **put back** into the atmosphere by:
  – plants and animals **respiring**
  – bacteria and fungi in soil respiring when they **decompose** organisms
  – **burning** fossil fuels such as coal and oil
  – **erupting** volcanoes and forest fires.

- Carbon is also **recycled at sea**. The shells of marine organisms such as molluscs contain carbonates. When the organisms die their shells turn into a **sedimentary** rock called **limestone**. Limestone is attacked by **acid rain**, which weathers the rock, and carbon dioxide is released.

The nitrogen cycle

- **Nitrogen** is also recycled naturally. The atmosphere is 78% nitrogen. Plants and animals need nitrogen for growth, but can't use it directly because it is **unreactive**.

- **Decomposers** break down proteins in dead bodies and **urea** into **ammonia**. **Nitrifying bacteria** convert ammonia into **nitrates**.

- **Nitrogen-fixing bacteria** are found in soil or root nodules of plants such as beans. They 'fix' nitrogen by converting it into ammonia or nitrates and then into amino acids to form proteins.

- **Lightning** also fixes nitrogen by combining nitrogen and oxygen to form **oxides**. The oxides dissolve in rain and form nitrates in the soil.

- **Denitrifying bacteria** convert nitrates back into nitrogen gas.

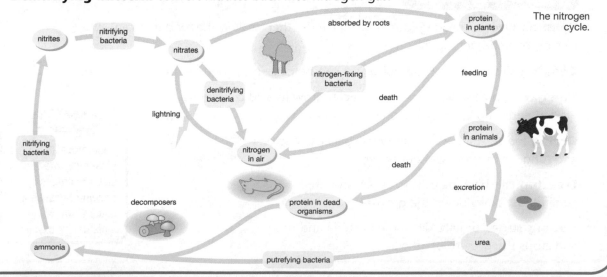

The nitrogen cycle.

Questions

1 Name the process that removes carbon from the atmosphere.

2 Explain how carbon is released from limestone.

3 Name the type of organism that converts protein into nitrates.

4 Describe one way in which nitrogen can be 'fixed'.

B4 Summary

Making food

Many plant cells contain **green chloroplasts**. Chloroplasts contain **chlorophyll**.

Chemical reactions in chloroplasts make **sugars**.

Photosynthesis takes place in **chloroplasts**.

Photosynthesis uses **carbon dioxide** and **water**.

Carbon dioxide enters through **stomata** in **leaves**.
Oxygen is released in photosynthesis.

Using water

Water can move in and out of cells.

Water inside cells keeps their shape.

Water can enter or leave by **diffusion** or **osmosis**.

Osmosis only works through a partially permeable membrane.

A plant **wilts** when it loses too much water.

Water enters plants through root hairs.

Phloem cells **carry dissolved food** to **roots**.

Xylem cells **carry water** up **stems**.

Water loss from plants is called **transpiration**.

Plants lose water through their **stomata**.

Transferring energy

Energy in plants and animals is transferred in **food chains** and **webs**.

Food chains rarely exceed five links.

Pyramids of biomass and number show different **trophic levels**.

Each trophic level 'loses' energy.

Pesticides can build up in food chains.

Intensive farming is very efficient.

The energy in **biomass** can be used as fuels called **biofuels**, for example to power buses.

Alcohol from fermenting sugar cane can be used as a biofuel.

Fast growing trees can fuel power stations.

Organic farming does not use manufactured chemicals.

Intensive farming uses **insecticides**, **herbicides** and **artificial fertilisers**.

Hydroponics is an example of intensive farming.

Decay and recycling

Carbon and **nitrogen** are recycled naturally.

Carbon dioxide is taken out of the air during **photosynthesis** and is put into the air during burning of fossil fuels and **respiration**.

Nitrogen is put into the air by **denitrifying bacteria** and is removed from the air by **nitrogen-fixing bacteria**.

Bacteria and **fungi** are **decomposers**.

The decay of food can be slowed down or stopped by methods of **food preservation**.

Food preservation methods slow down or stop the growth of bacteria and fungi.

Decomposers cause dead bodies to decay.

Decay is speeded up in warm, damp conditions.

In good shape

The advantages of an internal skeleton

- The human **internal skeleton** is better than an insect's **external skeleton** because:
  - it forms a framework for the body and grows along with the body
  - muscles can be easily attached and many joints give it flexibility
  - it is made of living tissue such as bone cells and blood cells.
- The long bones in arms and legs are hollow, so they are stronger and less likely to break than if they were solid. They have a main shaft with bone marrow inside that contains blood vessels. At each end is the head, which is covered with cartilage.

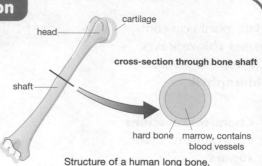

Structure of a human long bone.

D–C

Repair and growth of bone

- Moving someone with a suspected broken bone is dangerous. Nerves could be damaged, which, if their spine is broken, could result in paralysis.
- Microorganisms can infect broken bones or damaged cartilage. However, bone and cartilage can quickly grow and repair themselves.
- Before humans are born, their bones are all made of cartilage. As we grow, calcium and phosphorus are deposited in the bones making them hard. This process is called **ossification**. The amount of cartilage still present on bone can be used to determine the age of a skeleton.

B–A*

Bones, joints and levers

- The bones of elderly people are more easily broken as they are much softer due to **osteoporosis**.
- The hip is a ball and socket joint and the knee is a hinge joint. These are **synovial** joints because they contain **synovial fluid**.
- The biceps and triceps muscles in the arm are **antagonistic muscles**. They work together to move the arm. As one muscle contracts the other relaxes.

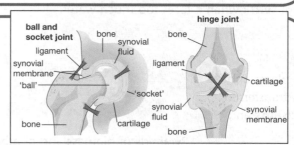

Two types of joints. The hinge joint can move only up or down. The ball and socket joint can rotate in almost all directions.

D–C

- Synovial fluid in joints absorbs shock and acts as a lubricant.
- Cartilage also helps to absorb shock. Ligaments connect bones preventing dislocations.
- Artificial knee and hip replacements are now common operations that enable patients to enjoy active, pain-free lives. However, there is a danger of rejection and infection.
- Arm movement is an example of a lever. The elbow acts as a fulcrum (pivot). As the biceps muscle contracts, it exerts an upwards force on the arm bones. Although the muscle contracts for only a short distance, the hand moves much further.

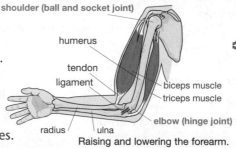

Raising and lowering the forearm.

B–A*

Questions

Grades D-C

1 Which type of tissue covers the head of a long bone?

Grades B-A*

2 What name is given to the process of replacing cartilage with bone?

Grades D-C

3 The biceps and triceps are antagonistic muscles. Explain why.

Grades B-A*

4 The bending of an arm is an example of a lever. Explain why.

The vital pump

Closed circulatory systems and the heart

D–C

- Fish have a **single circulatory system**. The blood goes around a single circuit.

- Humans have a **double circulatory system**. The blood goes round two circuits, from the heart to the lungs and from the heart to the rest of the body.

- The heart has four chambers, two upper atria and two large lower ventricles. Its main blood vessels are: aorta, vena cava, pulmonary artery and pulmonary vein.

- As blood flows from arteries, through arterioles (small arteries), capillaries and veins, the pressure decreases. The high blood pressure in arteries is caused by the heart muscles contracting to force the blood around the body.

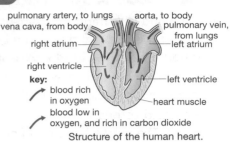

Structure of the human heart.

Top Tip!

To identify the parts of the heart correctly, practice labelling a diagram.

Circulation and the cardiac cycle

B–A*

- The heart in a single circulatory system has two chambers.

- The heart in a double circulatory system has four chambers; one side with deoxygenated blood and the other with oxygenated blood.

- Galen was the first doctor to realise the medical importance of the pulse, but he believed that the liver made blood, which was then pumped backwards and forwards around the body by the heart.

- William Harvey explained that the heart had four chambers. He knew that the blood travelled through arteries and veins, and thought they were joined by tiny blood vessels. Microscopes at that time were not good enough for him to see the capillaries.

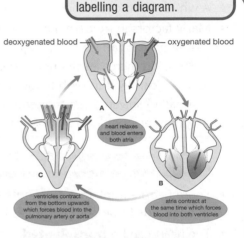

The cardiac cycle.

Heart rate

Top Tip!

Use the workbook to practice interpreting data on an echocardiogram.

D–C

- When you exercise, your heart rate increases supplying more blood containing oxygen and food to the muscles.

- Heart rate is controlled automatically. Small groups of cells called the **pacemaker** produce a small electric current. This stimulates the heart muscles and it contracts.

- Doctors can check the heart using:

  – an ECG (**electrocardiogram**) to record the nerve impulses in the heart

  – an **echocardiogram**, which uses ultrasound to produce pictures of the working heart.

- An artificial pacemaker can be used to send electrical impulses to the heart to regulate heartbeat.

- Hormones such as adrenaline can increase the heart rate.

B–A*

- The sino-atrial node (**SAN**) group of cells generates electrical impulses that spread across the atria causing them to contract. When the impulses reach the atrio-ventricular node (**AVN**), more impulses spread across the ventricles so they also contract.

Questions

(Grades D-C)

1 Where does the pulmonary artery take the blood to?

(Grades B-A*)

2 Describe the cardiac cycle of the human heart.

(Grades D-C)

3 What is the job of an artificial pacemaker?

(Grades B-A*)

4 What is the job of the SAN pacemaker?

Running repairs

Functions of the blood and health

- Red blood cells transport oxygen attached to a pigment called **haemoglobin**. White blood cells protect the body from infection by engulfing bacteria. Platelets are cell fragments that play an important part in **blood clotting**. Plasma carries dissolved substances such as glucose.
- At birth, a hole can be left between the left and right side of the heart. This 'hole in the heart' means blood leaving the heart carries less oxygen. Open-heart surgery can repair the heart wall.
- A blocked coronary artery prevents oxygen reaching the heart muscles and can cause a heart attack. The blocked artery can be by-passed using veins taken from other parts of the body.
- Doctors use '**heart-assist**' devices to help pump the blood and reduce the work done by the damaged heart muscles while they recover.
- If heart valves become damaged, some blood can flow back into the atria reducing blood pressure. The valves can be replaced by artificial valves.

D–C

- A red blood cell has a large surface area and no nucleus so it can absorb more oxygen.
- A white blood cell can change shape so it is able to surround and destroy bacteria.
- Many factors in modern life can contribute to a poor circulatory system.
  - A fatty diet can lead to a high level of **cholesterol** in the blood, which can block arteries.
  - Smoking increases the risk of heart disease.
  - Stress can lead to high blood pressure and a higher risk of a stroke or kidney damage.
  - Inhaling solvents can trigger a heart attack and injecting drugs can cause infections.
  - A high alcohol intake can lower blood pressure and affect blood clotting.

B–A*

Organ donation and blood clotting

- Some people think that carrying a donor card should be compulsory. Other people do not want donor cards to be compulsory as they do not want parts of their body removed.
- The heart can be **transplanted**. The tissue type must match the patient's heart to minimise **rejection**.
- **Haemophilia** is an inherited condition in which the blood does not easily clot.
- Substances in the diet such as vitamin K (green vegetables and cranberries are a good source) are important for the blood to clot.
- Doctors use drugs such as warfarin, heparin and aspirin to prevent clotting in people in danger of clot formation inside their blood vessels.
- When blood is donated, the blood group (A, B, AB, O) is recorded to make sure that when the donated blood is used in a **transfusion**, it does not react with the patient's own blood.
- The process of blood clotting involves many steps.
- Mixing different blood groups causes clumping (**agglutination**). The blood group depends on **agglutinins**. Antibody anti-A causes red blood cells containing antigen A to agglutinate.

D–C

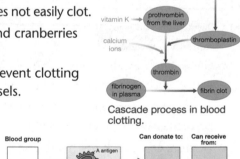
Cascade process in blood clotting.

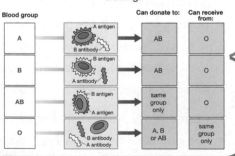
Blood group agglutinins.

B–A*

Questions

Grades D-C

1 Describe one way to solve the problem of damaged heart valves.

Grades B-A*

2 Describe the effects of alcohol on blood pressure.

Grades D-C

3 Suggest one reason why donor cards should be made compulsory.

Grades B-A*

4 Someone with blood group O cannot receive group A blood. Explain why.

Breath of life

Lung capacity

D–C

- The **total lung capacity** of adult human lungs is about 5 dm^3 of air. **Tidal air** is the amount of air moving in and out of the lungs when resting.
- The **vital capacity** is the largest amount of air that can be breathed out. The **residual capacity** is a small amount of air that we cannot breathe out.
- Breathing in and out uses muscles.
- Frogs' skin and fish gills need to be immersed in water to allow oxygen to diffuse into their blood. This means these animals are restricted to certain habitats.

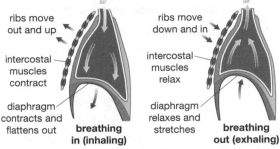

ribs move out and up — intercostal muscles contract — diaphragm contracts and flattens out — **breathing in (inhaling)**

ribs move down and in — intercostal muscles relax — diaphragm relaxes and stretches — **breathing out (exhaling)**

Inhaling (breathing in) and exhaling (breathing out), showing a side view of the chest.

Structure related to function

B–A*

- Human lungs are efficient gas exchangers. Air sacs have bulges called **alveoli** which increase the surface area for the exchange of oxygen and carbon dioxide, and have a moist surface and a thin lining to aid diffusion of gases into and out of the many blood capillaries.
- Fish gills are also very efficient: oxygen dissolved in water passes over many fine **gill filaments** that have a large surface area and a rich blood supply.

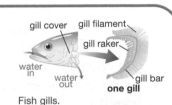

gill cover — gill filament — gill raker — water in — water out — gill bar — **one gill**

Fish gills.

Top Tip!

More information about alveoli can be found in B3 'Diffusion'.

Increasing transpiration

D–C

- Cells in the lungs make sticky mucus that traps dust particles and some bacteria.
- The lining of the trachea and bronchioles is covered by millions of tiny hair-like structures called **cilia** that produce a wave-like motion. This carries the mucus and any trapped dust upwards out of the lungs and into the throat.
- **Asbestosis** is an industrial disease caused by breathing in fine asbestos fibres. The fibres become trapped in the air sacs; this limits the exchange of gases.
- **Cystic fibrosis** is an inherited condition. Too much mucus is produced in the bronchioles, which means that the patient struggles to get enough oxygen.
- Poor lifestyle choices, such as smoking, are linked to **lung cancer**. In cancer, cells divide out of control, which reduces the surface area of the alveoli and eventually destroys lung tissue.
- **Asthma** is a condition which causes shortness of breath and wheezing. It can be treated using an inhaler that contains Ventolin, which widens the bronchioles making it easier to breathe.

B–A*

- The air sacs in the lungs are a 'dead end'. Any debris that is not removed by mucus and cilia remains, covering and irritating the cells lining the alveoli. These cells are easily damaged, which explains why there are so many diseases of the respiratory system.
- Asthma is believed to be a result of a combination of inherited, environmental, infectious and chemical factors. Complex responses all lead to less oxygen being available for gas exchange.

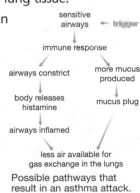

sensitive airways ← trigger → immune response → airways constrict → body releases histamine → airways inflamed; more mucus produced → mucus plug → less air available for gas exchange in the lungs

Possible pathways that result in an asthma attack.

Questions

Grades D–C

1 What happens to the intercostal muscles when you breathe in?

Grades B–A*

2 Fish gills are adapted for efficient gas exchange. Describe an adaptation.

Grades D–C

3 Asbestos is no longer used to insulate buildings. Explain why.

Grades B–A*

4 Describe what happens to mucus production during an asthma attack.

Waste disposal

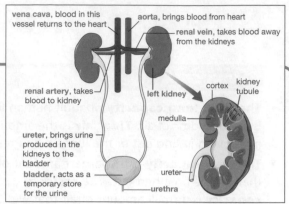

The structure of the kidneys.

Kidney structure and function

D–C

- The renal artery brings blood containing waste substances to the kidneys. **Urea** is a waste substance made in the liver from unwanted amino acids.

- The kidneys filter the blood under high pressure, removing the waste. Useful substances are reabsorbed back into the blood. **Urine** is the liquid waste from the kidneys.

- If you drink large amounts of liquid you will make large amounts of urine.

- If you do more exercise or it is hot, more water is lost as sweat, so less is lost as urine.

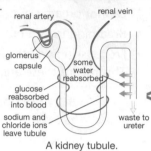

A kidney tubule.

B–A*

- A kidney contains about half a million kidney tubules. The **glomerulus** filters useful and waste materials from the blood. In the next part of the tubule the blood selectively reabsorbs useful substances such as glucose and water. Part of the tubule also regulates the body's levels of water and salt.

- If a kidney stops working, a **dialysis machine** can be used to act as an artificial kidney removing urea from the blood. Since urea molecules are small they diffuse through the membrane. The dialysis fluid is like normal blood plasma so the levels of sodium and glucose in the blood are maintained.

Temperature, carbon dioxide and water balance

D–C

Top Tip!

Urea is made in the liver. **Urine** is made in the kidney.

- Sweating helps the body to regulate its temperature and is an example of **homeostasis**. Water molecules in sweat use heat energy from the skin to change state from a liquid to a gas by evaporation. Thus the skin is cooled down. About 10 cm^3 of evaporating sweat can use 6 joules of energy from the skin.

- Exercising produces more energy from the oxidation of food, so more sweat is produced to keep the body temperature constant.

- More carbon dioxide, which must be removed, is also produced when exercising. Carbon dioxide reacts with water in the blood plasma forming carbonic acid which would upset the pH level of the blood If it was not removed. Thus a higher rate of breathing not only takes in more oxygen, it also gets rid of more carbon dioxide waste.

B–A*

Control of water reabsorption by ADH.

- **Anti-diuretic hormone** (**ADH**) made in the pituitary gland in the brain controls the reabsorption of water.

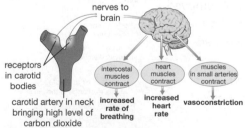

Control of carbon dioxide levels in the blood.

- A **negative feedback** mechanism ensures the correct water balance in the blood. The correcting mechanism (ADH production) is switched off when conditions return to normal.

- Carbon dioxide levels are also controlled.

Questions

(Grades D–C)

1 Which organ in the body makes urea?

(Grades B–A*)

2 Reabsorption of glucose uses active transport. Suggest a reason why.

(Grades D–C)

3 Sweating cools down the body. Explain why.

(Grades B–A*)

4 Describe the processes involved in producing more dilute urine.

Life goes on

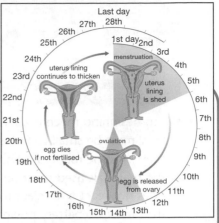

The female menstrual cycle.

The menstrual cycle

- The **menstrual cycle** is the cycle of stages in the female that produces eggs.
- **Ovulation** is the release of an egg around the middle of the cycle.
- The uterus lining becomes thicker, which helps a fertilised egg to embed in it.
- **Menstruation**, the release of the broken down cells from the uterus lining, occurs if an egg is not fertilised or does not become embedded.

Hormonal control of the menstrual cycle

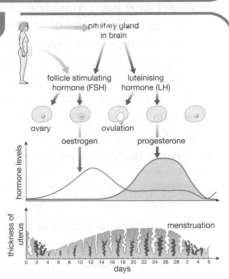

How hormones control the menstrual cycle.

- The menstrual cycle is controlled by hormones and is triggered by receptors in the hypothalamus in the brain that cause the **pituitary gland** to produce:
  - **follicle stimulating hormone** (**FSH**), which stimulates an egg to start developing
  - **luteinising hormone** (**LH**), which controls the release of an egg.
- As the follicle in the ovary develops, it releases varying amounts of **oestrogen** and **progesterone**. These hormones control the growth of uterus cells and thus the thickness of the uterus lining.
- If an egg is fertilised, the levels of progesterone remain high and no FSH is produced. So no more eggs develop and the uterus lining does not break down.

Infertility and foetal screening – treatment and ethics

- If the ovaries do not develop eggs, injections of FSH can be given.
- *In-vitro* ('in glass') fertilisation (**IVF**) treatment is when the egg is fertilised outside the body. Sometimes the fertilised egg can be implanted into a **surrogate** mother.
- Some women cannot produce eggs, so they rely on 'egg donations' for IVF treatment.
- If the oviducts are blocked or a husband has a low sperm-count, artificial insemination can be carried out. The husband's sperm (or donated sperm) is put directly into the uterus.
- The development of a foetus is checked regularly throughout pregnancy.
  - A simple blood test identifies a high risk of certain birth defects including chromosome abnormalities such as Down's syndrome and genetic disorders such as cystic fibrosis.
  - **Amniocentesis**. A thin needle is guided by ultrasound through the abdomen into the amniotic fluid that surrounds the foetus. A sample of fluid and loose cells is taken.
- Injections of FSH are straightforward and can be used without major side-effects.

- Surrogate mothers may become emotionally attached to the developing baby during pregnancy and then find it difficult to hand over the baby.
- IVF does not have a very high success rate. Multiple births are still a problem since more than one fertilised egg is used to try to ensure success.
- Amniocentesis carries a risk of causing miscarriage. If the test is positive, the parents face the difficult decision of whether to proceed with their pregnancy.

Questions

Grades D–C

1 Describe what happens to the uterus on day one of the menstrual cycle.

Grades B–A*

2 What is the role of LH in the menstrual cycle?

Grades D–C

3 During amniocentesis loose cells are taken. Suggest why.

Grades B–A*

4 Describe one argument against IVF treatment.

New for old

Mechanical replacements

- When designing mechanical replacements, many things have to be considered:
  - they must be small to fit inside the body or to be carried
  - they must be made of lightweight but strong materials
  - the materials used must be inert so the body does not react and reject them
  - they must be battery powered so the patient can move around.

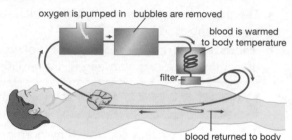

oxygen is pumped in   bubbles are removed
blood is warmed to body temperature
filter
blood returned to body

How a heart and lung machine works.

- **Heart and lung machines** are used during heart operations. The heart is stopped and cooled to reduce its oxygen use. The machine oxygenates the blood and returns it to the body while the surgeon operates on the resting heart.
- An iron lung which alters the air pressure around the chest can be used when a patient's chest muscles are paralysed. An increase in pressure forces air into the lungs; a decrease in pressure sucks air out of the lungs.
- **Kidney dialysis** machines are used to filter the blood if you have a kidney problem.

Ethics and success rates

- Some patients and their families may find it difficult to accept that:
  - the patient has a mechanical or biological replacement part
  - surgical procedures will be carried out on the dead body of the **donor**
  - someone's death has been necessary to provide the transplant.
- Many people are now happy to accept that, when they die, their organs and tissues will help others.
- Advances and experience in new medical techniques are steadily improving organ transplant success rates.

Donors and rejection

- There are thousands of people on a list waiting for a transplant operation.
- The waiting list is caused by:
  - a shortage of donors, especially with the right size of organs and a similar age to recipients
  - tissues or blood not matching.
- Living donors can donate one kidney, blood and bone marrow. Their tissues and blood must match a recipient.
- A person that is 'brain dead' (irreversible loss of consciousness and inability to breathe unaided due to damage to the brain stem), can donate organs and tissues for transplantation. If they die from cardio-respiratory failure, only their tissues will be used.
- The NHS Organ Donor Register is an 'opt in' system that has been used for 10 years. People over 18 years old can register their approval to use their organs after death.
- After a transplant, **immuno-suppressive** drugs will be needed. This is because the body's immune system reacts to 'foreign' tissue and rejects it.

Questions

Grades D-C

1 Explain why mechanical replacements must be inert.

Grades B-A*

2 Organ transplants are now more successful. Suggest one reason why.

Grades D-C

3 Write down one reason for the long transplant waiting list.

Grades B-A*

4 Explain why **immuno-suppressive** drugs are needed after a transplant.

Size matters

Growth checks

D–C

- Organisms divide their cells by a type of division called **mitosis**, which makes new identical cells so the organism can grow.

- A **health visitor** regularly checks a baby's growth by measuring and recording it's length, mass and head size.

- These measurements are recorded on **growth charts** to check that the baby's growth is within the normal range.

- Any abnormal measurements indicate growth problems and further medical advice is needed.

- Growth charts are only a guide. In the future, with better understanding of diet and environmental factors, the average height and mass could increase and the charts will need to be modified.

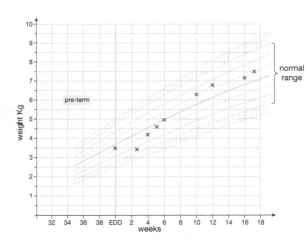

Growth charts for a baby boy's mass up to 18 weeks after birth.

Growth and life expectancy

D–C

- Your diet must contain proteins for muscle growth, and calcium and vitamin D for bone growth.

- Regular exercise makes the body release more **growth hormones**.

- Some people are very small (**dwarfs**) and some very tall (**giants**). The main causes are either hereditary or the wrong amount of growth hormone.

- People have a longer life expectancy than their ancestors did due to:
  - modern treatments and cures for many diseases
  - fewer deaths from industrial diseases
  - healthier diet and lifestyle
  - better housing conditions.

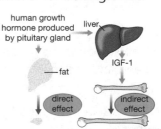

Hormone control of growth.

B–A*

- The **human growth hormone** is produced by the pituitary gland in the brain. It has two main effects:
  - a direct effect of stopping fat being stored and releasing it for energy and growth
  - an indirect effect of stimulating the liver to produce another hormone (**IGF-1**). This hormone triggers an increased production of cartilage causing an increase in length of the long bones in the arms and legs.

- Here are some ideas on life expectancy that you may share. Can you think of any others?

'I don't want to grow old and be unhealthy. I will not be able to enjoy myself or move around. I will just be a burden to other people and have to stay in hospital or a nursing home. Doctors will spend time and money just keeping me alive.'

'I want to live as long as possible. Life is precious. I can enjoy being alive even if I am ill or confined to a bed. My life is just as important as other people's.'

Questions

Grades D-C
1 What is the normal weight range for a boy aged 16 weeks?

Grades D-C
2 Regular exercise can help with better growth. Explain why.

Grades D-C
3 Suggest one reason why we expect to live longer than our ancestors.

Grades B-A*
4 What effect does IGF-1 have on the body?

B5 Summary

Bones and joints

We have an **internal skeleton**.

Bones are moved by muscles contracting.

A **synovial joint** is lubricated by **synovial fluid**.

Broken bones can repair themselves.

Breathing, respiration and excretion

The diaphragm and intercostal muscles help us breathe.

We have a four-chambered heart.

The kidneys filter blood at high pressure.

A, B, AB and O are different blood groups. These blood groups can react with each other because of **agglutinins**.

Sweat and **urine** are excreted from the body.

ADH is used to control the amount of water excreted by the kidney.

Growth, repair and reproduction

Fertilisation is the fusion of an egg and sperm.

New cells are produced by **mitosis**.

Dwarfs and giants can be a result of their genes or hormonal imbalance.

Many body parts can have **biological** or **mechanical replacements**.

Heart **transplants** and **heart-assist devices** can treat serious heart problems.

Growth can be measured as an increase in height or mass.

The **menstrual cycle** is controlled by hormones. **oestrogen**, **progesterone**, **FSH** and **LS**.

There are many different treatments for **infertility**.

People have to wait a long time for transplants because there is a shortage of donors.

Understanding bacteria

Bacterial shape and reproduction

- Bacteria are made up of three main parts.

part	function
flagellum	helps bacterium to move
cell wall	helps bacterium keep its shape and prevents bursting
bacterial DNA	controls bacterium cell and helps it reproduce

- Bacterial cells are different to animal and plant cells. They do *not* have:
  - a nucleus
  - mitochondria
  - vacuole
  - chloroplasts.
- Bacteria are used to make things such as yoghurt.
- The bacteria are placed in large **fermenters** so they can grow in number using a type of **asexual reproduction** called **binary fission**; they keep splitting into two.

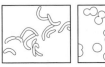

curved rod   spherical   spiral   rod

Bacteria can be classified according to their shape.

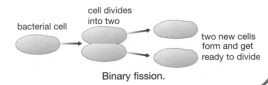

Binary fission.

How bacteria feed

- Most bacteria feed on organic nutrients such as carbohydrates and proteins but some can make their own food. They use chemicals such as hydrogen sulphide or ammonia to make organic nutrients.
- Using many different energy sources enables bacteria to live in a wide range of habitats.
- Bacteria reproduce so fast it is difficult to stop them. The food they grow on quickly spoils and can become dangerous to eat.
- If harmful bacteria get inside our bodies they can reproduce, causing diseases such as typhoid.

Making yoghurt

- There are five main stages in the production of yoghurt:
  - all the equipment is **sterilised** and the milk is pasteurised by heating to 95 °C for 20 minutes, then cooled to 46 °C
  - bacterial **culture** is added and the milk is **incubated** at 46 °C for about 5 hours
  - samples are taken to find out when the yoghurt is ready
  - flavours and colours are added
  - the yoghurt is cooled and packaged.

Handling bacteria

- When using bacteria it is always good practice to follow some strict rules:
  - wash hands before and after handling bacteria
  - disinfect working areas
  - sterilise all equipment before and after use
  - never leave the lids off containers.

Questions

1 Why do bacteria have flagella?

2 Write down the name of a chemical that bacteria can use to make food.

3 When making yoghurt, milk is first heated to 95 °C. Suggest why.

4 Describe one example of good practice when using bacteria.

Harmful microorganisms

Pathogens

- Microorganisms that cause diseases are called **pathogens**. They get inside our bodies where they reproduce, making us ill.

  - Eating food infected with bacteria causes **food poisoning**.

  - Drinking water infected with cholera bacteria causes **cholera**.

  - A protozoan that lives in water causes **dysentery**.

  - If a person with **influenza** sneezes, the virus is passed on when someone else breathes in the contaminated air.

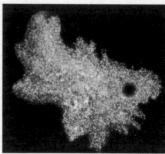

Protozoa cause dysentery.

- Infectious diseases take some time to go through all their stages:

  - first the microorganism enters the body

  - it then reproduces to build up numbers; the **incubation period**

  - the microorganism starts to make harmful **toxins**

  - symptoms start to appear, such as fever.

- Bacteria such as *Salmonella* and *E. coli* that cause food poisoning live on food. Cooking food correctly will kill them.

- *Vibrio cholerae* which causes cholera and *Entamoeba* which causes dysentery both live in water. Boiling water before it is drunk will destroy them.

Top Tip!

In the exam you will be asked to interpret data on food poisoning, cholera, dysentery and septicaemia. Use past papers and the workbook to practice this type of question.

The problem diseases and finding cures

- After natural disasters, diseases such as dysentery, cholera and food poisoning become a big problem.

- Pioneering work by scientists has reduced the spread of some diseases.

  - Louis **Pasteur** proved that microorganisms in the air caused food to go bad.

  - Joseph **Lister** invented the first **antiseptic**. He used carbolic acid to stop wounds becoming infected.

  - Alexander **Fleming** discovered the first **antibiotic** – **penicillin** – a mould that stops bacteria growing.

The rapid spread of diseases

- Disease will spread very easily after a natural disaster because:

  - sewage systems and water supplies become damaged

  - electrical supplies are lost causing food to decay

  - the health service is disrupted.

Questions

(Grades D-C)

1 Describe how you could become infected with the dysentery pathogen.

(Grades B-A*)

2 Which two bacteria cause food poisoning?

(Grades D-C)

3 Write down the name of the first antibiotic.

(Grades B-A*)

4 Explain why loss of electrical supplies could cause food poisoning.

Microorganisms – factories for the future?

Fermentation and cleaning water

D–C

- Fermentation is **anaerobic respiration** in yeast; it occurs without oxygen.

  sugar ⟶ alcohol + carbon dioxide + energy

- Dried yeast placed in sugar solution grows very slowly initially, then it grows rapidly. For **optimum growth**, yeast needs the correct conditions:
  - availability of food
  - optimum temperature
  - optimum pH
  - removal of product.

- Water used to clean the equipment used in food production becomes contaminated with sugar. Yeast is added to the water to break down the sugar into alcohol, which is removed so the water can be safely returned to rivers.

Yeast and respiration

B–A*

- The overall balanced chemical equation for fermentation is:

  $$C_6H_{12}O_6 \longrightarrow 2C_2H_5OH + 2CO_2 + energy$$

- If yeast is provided with plenty of oxygen it carries out **aerobic respiration**, converting glucose into carbon dioxide and water. To ensure yeast produces alcohol, it must be grown in the absence of oxygen.

- The growth rate of yeast will double for every 10 °C rise in temperature until the optimum temperature is reached, above which the yeast cells start to die.

Brewing beer

D–C

- The main stages in brewing beer include:
  - extracting sugar from malted barley and adding hops to give a beer flavour
  - heating the mixture to kill unwanted microorganisms
  - cooling the mixture before adding the yeast and keeping it warm while it ferments
  - **clarifying** the beer to leave a clear liquid
  - **pasteurising** the beer to kill unwanted microorganisms and putting it into bottles or casks.

- Wine is made in a similar way using grapes instead of hops and barley.

- To increase the alcohol content of **spirits**, the alcohol is separated from the water by **distillation**. The mixture is heated to evaporate the alcohol, which is then cooled to turn it back into a liquid. It is legal to brew beer for your own use at home, but spirits have to be distilled on licensed premises.

B–A*

- To preserve beer, **pasteurisation** is used. Brewers heat the beer to 72 °C for 15 seconds before it is bottled.

- The many different varieties or strains of yeast each give the beer or wine a different flavour.

- Alcohol kills yeast when it reaches a certain level. Different yeasts can tolerate different levels of alcohol – a greater tolerance produces higher levels of alcohol.

Questions

Grades D-C

1 Write down the word equation for fermentation.

Grades B-A*

2 Yeast grown to make alcohol is not given oxygen. Explain why.

Grades D-C

3 Describe how the alcohol concentration of a drink can be increased.

Grades B-A*

4 How can wines be made with different flavours?

Biofuels

Biogas production

- Marshes, septic tanks and even our own digestive systems produce biogas.
- Biogas usually contains:
  - about 60% methane
  - about 40% carbon dioxide
  - traces of hydrogen, nitrogen and hydrogen sulphide gas.
- To make methane, waste is fed into the digester continuously. The solids that remain are regularly removed through the outlet tank.
  This is a **continuous flow method** because it carries on without stopping for months or years.
- Biogas production increases as temperature increases, up to about 45 °C. Above this, production slows down.

inner tank   gas holder

organic waste enters here

gas to house for heating/lighting

outlet tank

digestion vessel

ground

Continuous flow method of making methane.

Important facts about biogas

- To burn easily the biogas needs to contain more than 50% methane, but care must be taken when using it. A mixture of as little as 10% methane in the air can be explosive.
- Different types of bacteria are needed to produce methane.
- Temperature affects biogas production. As the temperature increases, the bacteria multiply faster and the enzymes within them work better. Above 45 °C, the enzymes are denatured and the bacteria die.

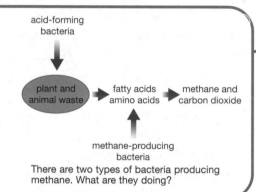

acid-forming bacteria

plant and animal waste → fatty acids amino acids → methane and carbon dioxide

methane-producing bacteria

There are two types of bacteria producing methane. What are they doing?

Uses, advantages and disadvantages of biofuels

- When biogas burns it releases energy. That energy can be used:
  - to generate electricity
  - to produce hot water and steam for central heating
  - as a fuel for buses.
- Biofuels such as gasohol and biogas have advantages:
  - they are an alternative to fossil fuels
  - burning biofuels only recycles the carbon dioxide used by plants (burning fossil fuels increases the levels of carbon dioxide in the air)
  - no **particulates** (fine particles like soot) are produced when they burn.

Top Tip!

Remember: biofuels still produce carbon dioxide. The advantage is that it is not from carbon that has been locked up for millions of years.

- Biogas is a much cleaner fuel than fossil fuels such as diesel and petrol, but as it is a mixture of gases, it contains less energy than natural gas.
- Biogas and other biofuels have advantages over fossil fuels:
  - fossil fuels are running out, so using biofuels means they will last longer
  - biofuels are a sustainable resource
  - biofuels do not increase atmospheric levels of the greenhouse gas carbon dioxide.

Questions

Grades D-C

1 Why is the method of making methane called a continuous flow method?

Grades B-A*

2 Digesters must be kept below 45 °C. Explain why.

Grades D-C

3 Describe how biogas can help run a central heating system.

Grades B-A*

4 Biofuels may help reduce the greenhouse effect. Explain why.

Life in soil

Earthworms and soil improvement

- Earthworms live in the soil and improve its structure and **fertility**. In fertile soil, plants get more minerals and grow better.
- Earthworms improve the soil by:
  - burrowing, which **aerates** the soil and improves **drainage**
  - eating and burrowing through the soil and mixing up its layers
  - taking organic material from the surface and burying it, which allows bacteria and fungi in the soil to decompose the material
  - adding chalk to the soil as it eats it, so **neutralising** acid soils.

Why do gardeners welcome earthworms?

- Charles Darwin realised that when earthworms mix up the layers, it makes a deeper layer of fertile soil. Soil can also be improved by:
  - aerating the soil so plants and animals have more oxygen for respiration
  - draining waterlogged soil to help plant roots get more oxygen
  - adding humus to sandy soil so it holds more water, which plants need for photosynthesis
  - adding lime to acidic soil to neutralise the acid.

Food webs and recycling

- There are many different animals in the soil all feeding off each other:
  - herbivores such as slugs, snails and wire worms all feed on plants
  - detritivores such as earthworms, millipedes and springtails all feed on dead organic matter
  - carnivores such as centipedes, spiders and ground beetles feed on other animals.

- Different types of bacteria living in the soil decompose dead animals and plants. This releases elements such as nitrogen back into the soil. Plants use this nitrogen for growth. Without bacteria, plants would run out of the elements they need.

- Nitrogen is an important element in the production of proteins. The **nitrogen cycle** depends on different types of bacteria:
  - **saprophytic soil bacteria** decompose dead animals and plants forming ammonia
  - **nitrifying bacteria**, such as **Nitrosomonas** and **Nitrobacter**, use nitrification to convert ammonia into soluble nitrates that plants can absorb
  - **nitrogen-fixing bacteria**, such as *Azotobacter* and *Clostridium* in the soil and *Rhizobium* in the root nodules of leguminous plants, convert nitrogen from the air for use in their proteins.

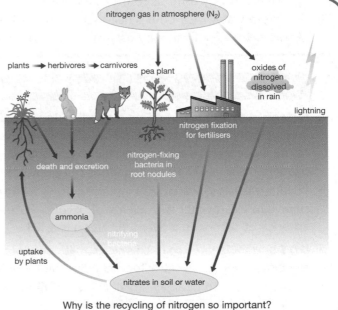

Why is the recycling of nitrogen so important?

Questions

1 Earthworms burrow into the soil. Explain why this improves the soil.

2 Why did Darwin believe earthworms were so important to soil?

3 Earthworms are detrivores; name another detrivore that lives in soil.

4 What is the job of *Azotobacter* in the nitrogen cycle?

Microscopic life in water

Life in water

- For organisms living in water, there are advantages and disadvantages:

advantages	disadvantages
plenty of water stops dehydration	it is difficult to maintain the water balance in their cells
in a large volume of water, the temperature changes little during the year	some find it difficult to move against the currents
they can grow bigger as water supports their weight	
excretion of waste, such as urea, is simple as it becomes diluted in the water	

- Frogs and some insects lay their eggs in water where their young can live and feed. The adults move on to land to find food, thus reducing the competition between the young and the adults.

- Phytoplankton photosynthesise. Their growth is limited by temperature, light and the availability of nitrates and phosphates. When the phytoplankton population goes up in the summer, so does the zooplankton population which feeds on them.

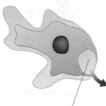

water enters continuously by osmosis

Removal of excess water in Amoeba.

- The cytoplasm of single-celled *Amoeba* is a concentrated solution of proteins and salts, but they live in fresh water that is more dilute. The excess water that moves into the *Amoeba* by **osmosis** is removed by **contractile vacuoles**.

energy is used to collect excess water in small vacuoles

small vacuoles merge to form a large contractile vacuole

the contractile vacuole bursts emptying its contents to the outside

- As salmon live in salt and fresh water, they have to change depending on where they are:
  - in salt water they drink water containing salt, so their gills secrete the salt back into the sea; water is lost by osmosis so they produce very concentrated urine
  - in fresh water their bodies need salt, so the gills actively transport salt into the body from the water; they gain water by osmosis so they produce large amounts of dilute urine.

Eutrophication, biological indicators and pollution

- **Eutrophication** is caused by phytoplankton called algae. Fertilisers from farm land or untreated sewage pollutes the water. Algae feed on the nutrients and their population grows rapidly. Many of the algae start to die, rot and fall to the bottom. Bacteria decompose the algae, using up the oxygen in the water. Animals cannot carry out respiration and die.

- Pollution levels in water are monitored using **biological indicators**. Caddis fly larvae can only survive in clean water with plenty of oxygen. Pollution can also change the pH of the water. The absence of salmon in a river indicates a low pH.

- **DDT** and **PCBs** are **toxic** chemicals that contaminate sea water. As they are not broken down in the body, they pass up the food chain so high levels build up in animals' bodies.

- Increased growth of algae, an algal bloom, tends to occur in summer when it is warmer and there is more light.

Questions

1 What advantages does living in two habitats give to frogs?

2 When does a salmon actively transport salt into its body?

3 Caddis fly larvae are not found in polluted water. Suggest a reason why.

4 Algal blooms are more common when there is more light. Explain why.

Enzymes in action

Different types of enzymes

- Different enzymes in biological washing powders remove different kinds of stains:
  - **amylases** remove stains that contain starch (a carbohydrate)
  - **lipases** break down fatty stains such as butter and grease
  - the enzyme group **proteases** digest proteins from blood stains.
- Enzymes are sensitive to pH and stop working if water is too acid or too alkali.
- **Sucrose** is the most common type of sugar used in food products. The enzyme **sucrase** is used to break it down to a much sweeter sugar that can be used by the food industry.

Top Tip!
Sucrase has another name – invertase.

- Insoluble stains are difficult to get out of clothes, so enzymes break them down into smaller soluble molecules which are easily washed away by water.

insoluble stain	enzyme	soluble molecule
carbohydrate	amylase	sugars
fats	lipase	fatty acids and glycerol
protein	protease	amino acids

- Sucrase breaks down sucrose into the sugars glucose and **fructose**.

$$\text{sucrose} \xrightarrow{\text{sucrase}} \text{glucose} + \text{fructose}$$

- Glucose and fructose are much sweeter than sucrose. This is useful for producing low-calorie food as less is needed to make the food sweet.

Top Tip!
Remember: enzymes speed up reactions without becoming part of the product.

The advantages of immobilising enzymes

- Most enzyme-catalysed reactions take place in a solution. It is difficult to separate the enzyme from the product. Immobilising the enzyme makes it is easier to separate it from the solution and prevents it contaminating the product.
- Alginate beads are useful in industries that use continuous flow processing where the substrates for a reaction are added to a container as fast as the products are removed. The immobilised enzymes remain inside the container and are used again and again.

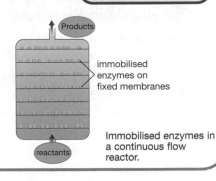

Products

immobilised enzymes on fixed membranes

reactants

Immobilised enzymes in a continuous flow reactor.

Lactose intolerance

- **Lactose** is a sugar found in milk. It needs to be digested before it can be absorbed into the blood. People with lactose intolerance lack the enzyme **lactase** that breaks lactose down into glucose and **galactose**, which is easier to digest.
- To produce lactose-free milk, immobilised lactase is added to milk.
- Adult cats lose the ability to digest lactose. Bacteria in their gut ferment the lactose resulting in diarrhoea and wind. Special cat milk is now produced using lactase.

Questions

Grades D-C
1 Which group of enzymes are needed to remove protein stains?

Grades B-A*
2 What are the products when sucrase breaks down sucrose?

Grades D-C
3 Write down two advantages of using immobilised enzymes.

Grades B-A*
4 What are the products when lactase breaks down lactose?

Genetic engineering

Transgenic organisms

- An organism altered by genetic engineering is called a **transgenic organism**.

- To make a transgenic organism, scientists:
  - identify the gene they need and remove it from the DNA
  - cut open the DNA in another organism
  - add the gene to the DNA of that organism; this is now a transgenic organism
  - clone the transgenic organism.

- **Restriction enzymes** are used to cut out the section of DNA.

- **Ligase** is an enzyme used to stick the DNA strands together.

- **Assaying** is used to find out if the gene has stuck in the bacteria. The bacteria are:
  - given a gene to make them resistant to antibiotics
  - spread on nutrient agar containing the antibiotic
  - checked; if they grow, the gene has stuck.

donor DNA

loops of bacterial DNA caled plasmids

plasmid DNA magnified

chosen gene

plasmid DNA cut with restriction enzyme

restriction enzyme action

restriction enzyme action

DNA cut with restriction enzyme

donor DNA joined into plasmid using ligase enzyme to make a recombinant plasmid

ligase enzyme action

recombinant plasmid is cloned and clones make human proteins

Steps in transferring a chosen human gene into a bacterial plasmid.

Making human insulin and improving crops

- Diabetics are people who cannot control their blood sugar levels because they do not make enough of the hormone **insulin**. Many diabetics need to inject insulin so the hormone has to be produced artificially. Large quantities can be produced using bacteria that contain the human gene for making insulin.

- Crops grown all over the world provide food. Countries with poor soil and little water need crops the most. Genetic engineering is used to:
  - increase crop yield   – make crops resistant to weed killers
  - make plants produce other chemicals, e.g. rice that produces vitamin A.

- Plants can be genetically engineered to:
  - make them grow bigger and faster
  - be resistant to disease
  - tolerate drought or salt water

- There are advantages and disadvantages to genetically engineered plants:
  - one advantage is that they could solve the world food shortage
  - one disadvantage is that some people think that GM food is not safe to eat.

Questions

(Grades D-C)

1 Describe the stages involved in creating a transgenic organism.

(Grades B-A*)

2 What are restriction enzymes used for?

(Grades D-C)

3 Which type of organism is genetically engineered to make insulin?

(Grades B-A*)

4 Suggest one disadvantage to growing plants resistant to weed killers.

B6 Summary

Bacteria

Bacteria are microscopic organisms. Some bacteria are harmful while others have many uses.

Bacteria can exploit a wide range of habitats.

Bacteria have different shapes:
– spherical   – spiral
– rod   – curved rod.

Bacteria are destroyed by **antibiotics**.

Bacteria cells lack:
– a true nucleus – chloroplasts
– motochondria   – vacuole

Microorganisms

Bacteria, fungi, protozoa and viruses are all microorganisms.

Food poisoning is caused by *Salmonella* and *E. coli* bacteria.

The bacteria *Vibrio* causes **cholera**.

Viruses can cause **influenza**.

Pasteur, **Fleming** and **Lister** all pioneered the treatment of diseases.

The protozoan *Entamoeba* causes **dysentery**.

Natural disasters cause a rapid spread in diseases.

The fungus, **yeast**, carries out **fermentation** to make alcohol, in the production of **beer**, **wine** and **gasohol**.

Beer is **pasteurised** to destroy unwanted bacteria.

Life in soil and water

Charles Darwin highlighted the importance of earthworms in agriculture.

Aerating and **draining** improves soil.

Phytoplankton and **zooplankton** live in water.

Sewage and fertiliser **pollution** can cause **eutrophication**.

Bacteria are involved in the **nitrogen cycle**.

Earthworms help to improve the structure and **fertility** of the soil.

PCBs and DDT build up in the food chain.

Enzymes are biological catalysts

Enzymes have everyday uses, such as stain removers in biological washing powders.

Enzymes can be **immobilised** to improve their use.

Lactase converts lactose to glucose and galactose.

Sucrase converts sucrose to glucose and fructose.

Genetic engineering

Genetic engineering involves taking genes from one organism and putting them into another.

Genetic engineering can be used to make **insulin** and improve crops.

How science works

Understanding the scientific process

As part of your Biology assessment, you will need to show that you have an understanding of the scientific process – How Science Works.

This involves examining how scientific data is collected and analysed. You will need to evaluate the data by providing evidence to test ideas and develop theories. Some explanations are developed using scientific theories, models and ideas. You should be aware that there are some questions that science cannot answer.

Collecting and evaluating data

You should be able to devise a plan that will answer a scientific question or solve a scientific problem. In doing so, you will need to collect data from both primary and secondary sources. Primary data will come from your own findings – often from an experimental investigation. While working with primary data, you will need to show that you can work safely and accurately, not only on your own but also with others.

Secondary data is found by research – often using ICT, but do not forget that books, journals, magazines and newspapers are also sources of secondary data. The data you collect will need to be evaluated for its validity and reliability.

Presenting information

You should be able to present your information in an appropriate, scientific manner. This means being able to develop an argument and come to a conclusion based on recall and analysis of scientific information. It is important to use both quantitative and qualitative arguments.

Changing ideas and explanations

Many of today's scientific and technological developments have both benefits and risks. The decisions that scientists make will almost certainly raise ethical, environmental, social or economic questions. Scientific ideas and explanations change as time passes and it is the job of scientists to validate these changing ideas.

In 1692, the British astronomer Edmund Halley (after whom Halley's Comet was named) suggested that the Earth consisted of four concentric spheres. He was trying to explain the magnetic field that surrounds the Earth. There was, he said, a shell about 500 miles thick, two inner concentric shells and an inner core. The shells were separated by atmospheres and each shell had magnetic poles. The spheres rotated at different speeds. He believed this explained why unusual compass readings occurred. He also believed that each of these inner spheres supported life which was constantly lit by a luminous atmosphere.

This may sound quite an absurd idea today, but it is the work of scientists for the past 300 years that has developed different models that are constantly being refined.

How science works

Science in the News

Assessment

Science in the News is intended as the main way in which the OCR Biology course assesses your understanding of How Science Works.

While some of you will continue to study science, many of you will have completed your science education by the time you have finished your GCSE course. It is important that you are able to meet any scientific challenge which arises in later life.

It is important that you realise when data or information is not presented in an accurate way. Think about what is wrong in this example based on a newspaper report.

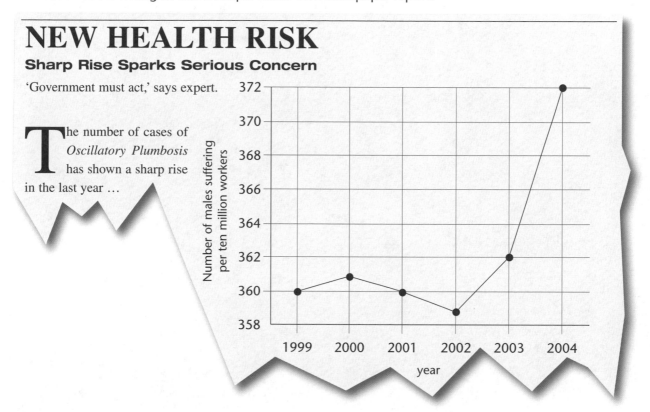

NEW HEALTH RISK
Sharp Rise Sparks Serious Concern

'Government must act,' says expert.

The number of cases of *Oscillatory Plumbosis* has shown a sharp rise in the last year …

Awareness of current issues

You should also be aware of what aspects of science may be important for people living in the 21st century.

One of the most controversial topics at this time is the extent to which stem cell research is permitted.

Your Science in the News assessment will ask you to undertake some research on a scientific issue. The task set to you will be in the form of a question. You will then have to produce a short report which will clearly show that you have

- considered both sides of the argument
- decided on the suitability, accuracy and/or reliability of the evidence
- considered the impact on society and the environment
- justified your conclusion about the question asked.

The aim is to equip you with life-long skills that will allow you to take a full and active part in the science of the 21st century.

Collins Revision

GCSE Higher Biology

Exam Practice Workbook

FOR OCR GATEWAY B

Fit for life

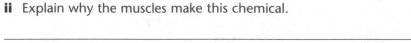

1 Ben goes running to get fit.

  a After a while Ben's muscles start to hurt.

    i Name the chemical made in Ben's muscles that causes the pain.

    _____ [1 mark]

    ii Explain why the muscles make this chemical.

    _____

    _____

    _____ [3 marks]

  b After the run Ben continues to breathe heavily and his heart rate stays high.
Explain why.

    _____

    _____

    _____ [2 marks]

2 Ben is an athlete and he is very fit. However, Ben still catches a cold.
Explain why being fit may not keep you healthy.

  _____

  _____ [2 marks]

3 Amelia has her blood pressure checked by a nurse. The nurse tells Amelia her blood pressure
is too high. She fills in a questionnaire for the nurse.

Blood pressure questionnaire			
Questions	Notes	Yes	No
1 Do you take regular exercise?	Strong heart muscles will lower blood pressure		✓
2 Do you eat a healthy balanced diet?	Reducing salt intake will lower blood pressure		✓
3 Are you overweight?	Being overweight by 5 kg raises blood pressure by 5 units	✓	
4 Do you regularly drink alcohol?	A high alcohol intake will damage liver and kidneys	✓	
5 Are you under stress?	Relaxation will lower blood pressure	✓	

  a Suggest **two** changes Amelia should make to lower her blood pressure.

    1 _____

    _____

    2 _____

    _____ [2 marks]

  b Describe the possible consequences of high blood pressure for Amelia.

    _____

    _____ [2 marks]

What's for lunch?

D–C

1 African children sometimes have a swollen abdomen, a condition caused by a low protein diet.

a Write down the name of this condition.

_____ [1 mark]

b A child has a mass of 40 kg. Calculate his recommended average protein intake (RDA) in grams. Use this formula: RDA in g = 0.75 x body mass in kg Show your working.

RDA = _____ g [2 marks]

2 Simon is overweight.

D–C

a Simon would like to lose weight. He decides to change his diet. Suggest **one other** way Simon could lose weight.

_____ [1 mark]

B–A*

b Simon is a vegetarian. He needs to think carefully about his protein intake. Explain why.

_____

_____

_____ [2 marks]

3 Enzymes are used to digest food.

D–C

a Finish the table to name the enzyme that digests each type of food and the product of the digestion. The first one has been done for you. [4 marks]

food type	enzyme	product
starch	carbohydrase	glucose
protein		
fat		

B–A*

b Use ideas about **enzymes**, **bile** and **size of droplets** to explain how fats are digested in the body.

_____

_____

_____

_____ [3 marks]

Keeping healthy

1 Look at the diagram. It shows how mosquitoes spread malaria.

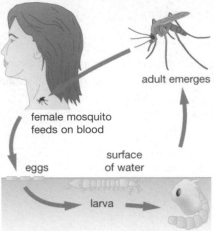

adult emerges

female mosquito feeds on blood

eggs

surface of water

larva

developing larva

a i What name is given to animals, such as the mosquito, that carry pathogens?

_____ [1 mark] **D–C**

ii Malaria is caused by a parasite called *Plasmodium falciparum*.
Explain why it is a parasite.

_____ [1 mark]

b Use the diagram to explain **one** way in which the spread of malaria could be controlled. **B–A***

_____
_____ [2 marks]

2 a Explain the difference between active and passive immunity. **D–C**

_____
_____
_____ [3 marks]

b Vaccinations can contain harmless forms of a pathogen. Vaccinations can cause active immunity. Explain how. **B–A***

_____
_____ [2 marks]

c Antibiotics are drugs used to treat some infections.

i Explain why antibiotics cannot be used to treat a viral infection. **D–C**

_____ [1 mark]

ii Suggest a reason why doctors are concerned about the over-use of antibiotics.

_____ [1 mark]

iii Doctors need to develop new drugs such as antibiotics. Describe how a blind trial can be used to test a new drug. **B–A***

_____
_____
_____ [2 marks]

Keeping in touch

1 a Finish the table to show which part of the eye performs which function.
The first one has been done for you.

[3 marks]

part of the eye	function
iris	*controls the amount of light entering the eye*
retina	
optic nerve	
cornea	

b The owl uses both eyes to see the same image.
Explain the advantage this type of vision gives the owl when it hunts.

_____

_____ [1 mark]

c Use ideas about **ciliary muscles**, **suspensory ligaments** and **lens** to
describe how the eye focuses on a distant object.

_____

_____

_____ [3 marks]

d Some people find it difficult to focus on distant objects because they are short-
sighted. Write down **two** different ways in which short sight can be corrected.

1 _____

2 _____ [2 marks]

---

2 The diagram shows the pathway taken by the impulse during an automatic reaction.

a Finish labelling the diagram to show the neurones involved in this process.

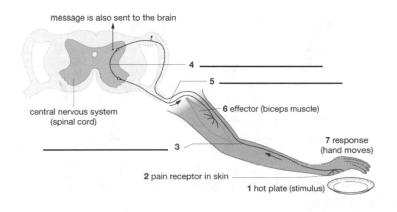

message is also sent to the brain

4 _____

5 _____

6 effector (biceps muscle)

central nervous system
(spinal cord)

_____ 3

7 response
(hand moves)

2 pain receptor in skin

1 hot plate (stimulus)

[3 marks]

b Describe how the impulse moves from one neurone to the next across the synapse.

_____

_____ [2 marks]

Drugs and you

1 a Different types of drugs have different effects. Finish the table by naming **one** example of each type of drug. Choose words from this list.

alcohol　　**anabolic steroid**　　**cannabis**　　**caffeine**　　**heroin**

type of drug	example
hallucinogen	
depressant	

[2 marks]

D–C

b Some people believe that personal use of cannabis should be allowed. Suggest **one** argument for and **one** argument against the legal use of cannabis.

For _____

_____

Against _____

_____

[2 marks]

B–A*

2 a Describe the effects of tobacco smoke on epithelial cells in the lining of the trachea.

_____

_____ [2 marks]

D–C

b Describe the effect of nicotine on synapses.

_____

_____ [2 marks]

B–A*

3 a The picture shows drinks that contain one unit of alcohol. Matthew drinks two pints of beer and a glass of whisky. Jo drinks three glasses of wine and a glass of whisky. Who drinks the most units? Explain your answer.

half pint beer　　single whisky　　glass of wine

_____

_____ [2 marks]

D–C

b There are more alcohol-related injuries ocurring on a Saturday compared to a Wednesday night. Suggest why.

_____

_____

_____ [2 marks]

B–A*

Staying in balance

D–C

1 a The body can lose or gain heat. If the body gets too hot you can suffer from dehydration. Explain why.

_____

_____ [2 marks]

b When the body gets too cold the pulse rate slows. Name the condition the body suffers from when it gets too cold.

_____ [1 mark]

B–A*

c To prevent the body getting too warm, vasodilation takes place. Explain what is meant by the term **vasodilation**.

_____

_____ [2 marks]

d Controlling body temperature involves negative feedback. Explain why.

_____

_____ [2 marks]

D–C

2 Blood sugar level is controlled by the hormone insulin.

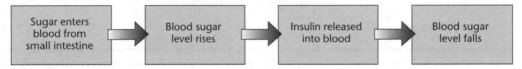

| Sugar enters blood from small intestine | → | Blood sugar level rises | → | Insulin released into blood | → | Blood sugar level falls |

a Some people do not make enough insulin. Write down the name of the condition they suffer from.

_____ [1 mark]

b Suggest **one** way such people can control their blood sugar level.

_____ [1 mark]

B–A*

3 This diagram shows the menstrual cycle.

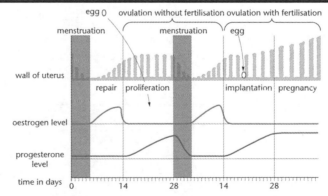

a Describe the effect of oestrogen on the lining of the uterus.

_____ [1 mark]

b Describe the effect of fertilisation on progesterone levels.

_____ [1 mark]

c Ovulation does not take place in some women. Suggest **one** way in which they can be treated.

_____ [1 mark]

Gene control

1 Finish the sentences about chromosomes.

Chromosomes are found in the _____ of the cell. They carry instructions called

_____. The chromosomes are made of a chemical called _____.   [3 marks]

2 The squirrel developed from a fertilised egg. The fertilised egg is made up of 20 chromosomes.

a How many chromosomes are in the egg before it is fertilised by a sperm?

_____ [1 mark]

b How many chromosomes are in one cell from the squirrel's ear?

_____ [1 mark]

c The nucleus of a human sperm is different from the nucleus of a squirrel sperm. Describe how they are different.

_____ [1 mark]

d The cells in the squirrel's ears contain a code to make insulin but only the squirrel's liver cells make insulin. Explain why.

_____

_____ [2 marks]

3 Chromosomes contain special chemicals called bases.

a How many different bases are there in a chromosome?

_____ [1 mark]

b If a section of chromosome contains 30 **T** bases, how many **A** bases will it contain? Explain your answer.

_____

_____ [2 marks]

c This diagram shows how DNA controls eye colour. Changing the DNA code would change the eye colour. Explain how.

_____

_____

_____

_____

_____

_____

_____

                    [3 marks]

NUCLEUS   CELL CYTOPLASM

DNA → copy of DNA to ribosomes

sequence of three bases decides amino acid

amino acids join together to make a protein such as an enzyme

enzyme controls a reaction such as making an eye pigment

Who am I?

1 We inherit different characteristics from our parents' chromosomes.

a Finish the table to show how gender is inherited. [4 marks]

egg	sperm	fertilised egg	gender of child
X	X		
X	Y		

b The sperm determine gender. Use your knowledge of genetics to explain this.

_____

_____

_____ [2 marks]

2 Mutations are changes to genes. Mutations can occur spontaneously or they can be caused by some other factors.

a Write down **one** factor that can cause mutations.

_____ [1 mark]

b Haemophilia is a condition caused by a gene mutation. A protein needed to clot the blood cannot be made by the body. Explain why the mutation stops the protein being made.

_____

_____ [2 marks]

3 a The diagram shows a breeding experiment.

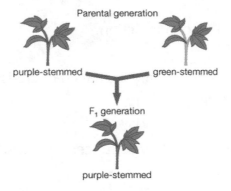

Parental generation

purple-stemmed — green-stemmed

F₁ generation

purple-stemmed

Which characteristic is dominant? Explain your answer.

_____ [1 mark]

b Cystic fibrosis is an inherited condition. Sam has cystic fibrosis but his parents are normal.

i Finish the genetic diagram to show how Sam inherited cystic fibrosis.

ii Put a (ring) around Sam's genotype on the diagram.

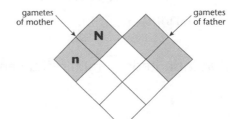

gametes of mother

gametes of father

N

n

[2 marks]

B1 Revision checklist

- I can explain the possible consequences of having high blood pressure. ☐

- I can state the word equation for respiration. ☐

- I know that religion, personal choice and medical issues can influence diet. ☐

- I can describe the main processes in digestion. ☐

- I can calculate BMI and RDA. ☐

- I can describe the role of antibodies and antigens in the defence against pathogens. ☐

- I can explain the difference between passive and active immunity. ☐

- I can describe the functions of the main parts of the eye. ☐

- I can describe the path of a reflex action. ☐

- I know the classification and effects of the different types of drugs. ☐

- I can interpret data on the effects of alcohol and smoking. ☐

- I can describe vasodilation and vasoconstriction. ☐

- I know that sex hormones cause secondary sexual characteristics, e.g. voice breaking and breast development. ☐

- I know that sex hormones can be used as contraceptives and for fertility treatment. ☐

- I know that chromosomes are made of DNA. ☐

- I can carry out a genetic cross to predict the possibilities of inherited disorders passing to offspring. ☐

- I know that inherited characteristics can be dominant or recessive. ☐

Ecology in our school grounds

D–C

1 a Clown fish are found in the coral reefs of the Pacific Ocean.

    i Suggest a reason why the clown fish are not found in British lakes.

_____ [1 mark]

    ii Suggest a reason why there are many undiscovered species in the Pacific Ocean.

_____ [1 mark]

B–A*

  b Wheat fields are artificial ecosystems and woods are natural ecosystems. Woods tend to have a higher biodiversity.

    i What is meant by the term **biodiversity**?

_____ [1 mark]

    ii Use your knowledge about invertebrates and vertebrates to explain how the use of pesticides could reduce the biodiversity of the wheat field.

_____

_____ [2 marks]

2 The following formula is used to estimate a population.

$$\frac{\text{number of animals caught first time} \times \text{number of animals caught second time}}{\text{number of marked animals caught second time}} = \text{population}$$

Researchers want to know the number of voles living in a wood. They set 30 traps in a small area of the wood and catch 20 voles. They mark the voles and then release them back into the wood. A week later they set more traps and catch 10 voles, five of them are marked.

D–C

  a Estimate the population of voles in the wood.

_____

_____ [2 marks]

B–A*

  b The researchers are not convinced that their estimate is correct.

    i Suggest **two** ways in which they can improve their method.

_____

_____ [2 marks]

    ii Explain why your suggestions would make the estimate more accurate.

_____

_____ [2 marks]

Grouping organisms

1 a The picture shows a penguin.

   i Finish this sentence.

   The penguin belongs to the vertebrate group

   called _____ .

[1 mark]

   ii Salmon belong to the vertebrate group called fish because they have scales. Explain why the penguin belongs to the group you have chosen.

_____

_____ [2 marks]

b Explain why spiders are invertebrates.

_____ [1 mark]

c This table compares animals and plants. Finish the table to describe animals.

	food	shape	movement
plants	*make own*	*spread out*	*stay in one place*
animals			

[3 marks]

---

2 A Zorse is a cross between two different species, a zebra and a horse.

a What name is used to describe a cross between two different species?

_____ [1 mark]

b Explain why the Zorse is difficult to classify.

_____ [1 mark]

---

3 The lion and tiger are different species.

a What is meant by the term **species**?

_____

_____ [2 marks]

b Lions and tigers belong to the same family of cats. This table shows the Latin names of different cats.

common name	Latin name
bobcat	*Felix rufus*
cheetah	*Acinonyx jubatus*
lion	*Panthera leo*
ocelot	*Felix pardalis*

[3 marks]

   i Two of these cats are more closely related than the others. Write down the **common** names of these **two** cats.

_____ and _____ [1 mark]

   ii What is the reason for your answer to part **b i**?

_____ [1 mark]

The food factory

1 Plants make glucose ($C_6H_{12}O_6$) by a process called photosynthesis.

   a Finish the balanced symbol equation for photosynthesis.

     _____ + _____ → $C_6H_{12}O_6$ + _____   [1 mark]

   b The products of photosynthesis have many uses. Finish the table to describe these uses. The first one has been done for you.

product of photosynthesis	use in the plant
glucose	*energy*
cellulose	
protein	
oil	

[3 marks]

2 Light can change the rate of photosynthesis.

   a Write down the names of **two other** factors that change the rate of photosynthesis.

     1 _____

     2 _____ _   [2 marks]

   b The graph shows the effect of light intensity on the rate of photosynthesis.

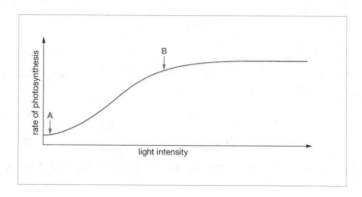

     i Describe the pattern shown in the graph.

     _____

     _____

     _____   [2 marks]

3 Glucose is a product of photosynthesis. The plant uses a process to release energy from glucose.

   a Write down the name of this process.

     _____   [1 mark]

   b Plants carry out this process 24 hours a day. Explain why.

     _____   [1 mark]

Compete or die

1 a The red and grey squirrels share the same ecological niche. What is meant by the term **ecological niche**?

_____ [1 mark]

b The red squirrel is native to Britain. The grey squirrel was introduced to Britain about 130 years ago. During the last 100 years grey squirrel numbers have increased and red squirrel numbers have decreased.

i Suggest a reason for the change in numbers.

_____ [1 mark]

ii Grey squirrels have been removed from the island of Anglesey. Suggest the effect this might have on the red squirrel population.

_____ [1 mark]

2 This is a diagram of a food chain.

a In one year the population of shrews decreases.

i Describe the effect this would have on the badger population.

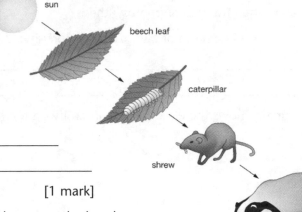

_____
_____

[1 mark]

ii In the same year the number of leaves on the beech tree decreases. Explain why.

_____
_____ [2 marks]

b The oxpecker feeds on the insects found on a buffalo's skin. The insects are called parasites.

i What is meant by the term **parasite**?

_____ [1 mark]

ii The oxpecker and the buffalo both benefit from the relationship. Write down the name given to this type of relationship.

_____ [1 mark]

3 Look at the graph. It shows the predator–prey relationship of lemmings and snowy owls. Write about how and why the number of lemmings change as indicated on the graph.

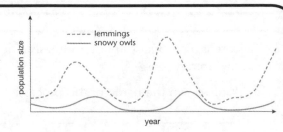

_____
_____

_____
_____ [3 marks]

Adapt to fit

1 a Look at the picture of a camel. The table shows how the camel is adapted to help it live in the desert. Finish the table by writing how these adaptations help it to survive. The first one has been done for you.

adaptation	why it helps the camel survive
large feet	*stop it sinking into sand*
no fat on body, except in hump	
hair-lined nostrils	
higher body temperatures do not harm camel	

[3 marks]

b Polar bears are adapted to live in the cold. They have thick fur for insulation as this stops them losing too much body heat.

   i Write about other ways they are adapted to live in the cold.

_____

_____

_____

_____

[3 marks]

   ii Polar bears are not in found in the same habitat as brown bears. Explain why. Use ideas about **competition** in your answer.

_____

_____

[2 marks]

2 a The cactus has spines instead of leaves. Explain why.

_____

_____ [2 marks]

b Lilies are pollinated by insects. Write down **one** adaptation of insect-pollinated flowers.

_____

[1 mark]

c Grasses are pollinated by wind. Descibe **two** ways they are from different insect-pollinated plants.

_____

_____ [2 marks]

Survival of the fittest

1 a Here are four sentences (**A–D**) about how the fossil of a dinosaur is formed. They are in the wrong order. Write the letters in the boxes to show the right order. The first one has been done for you.

A The dinosaur's hard parts were replaced by minerals.

B The dinosaur died.

C The dinosaur's soft tissue rotted away.

D The dinosaur became covered by sediment.

B			

[2 marks]

b The fossil record shows how living things have changed over time. The fossil record is incomplete. Explain why.

_____

_____ [2 marks]

c Creationists believe that each living thing was created individually and did not evolve. Use your knowledge about the fossil record to suggest **one** argument for and **one** argument against this theory.

For _____

_____

Against _____

_____ [2 marks]

D–C

B–A*

2 The following article gives information on the superbug MSRA. Read the article carefully and use it to help you answer the questions.

> **MRSA Where did it come from?**
> MRSA evolved because of natural selection. There are lots of different strains of the bacteria. Each strain has slightly different DNA. The DNA is also constantly mutating as the bacteria reproduce. Some of these mutations will be more resistant to antibiotics than others.
>
> When people take antibiotics, the less resistant strains die first, the more resistant strains are harder to destroy. If people stop taking the antibiotics too soon the resistant strains survive to reproduce and pass on their DNA. In this way, more and more strains evolve to be resistant to these new drugs.

a What is meant by the term **natural selection**?

_____ [1 mark]

b Use Darwin's theory of natural selection to explain how MRSA has evolved.

_____

_____ [2 marks]

D–C

B–A*

Population out of control?

D–C

1 a The rise in human population is causing an increase in the level of carbon dioxide in the air. Suggest **two** effects this increase may have on the environment.

1 _____

2 _____ [2 marks]

b The ozone layer in the Earth's atmosphere protects us from harmful ultraviolet rays. Chemicals are destroying the ozone layer.

i Write down the name of these chemicals.

_____ [1 mark]

ii The over-use of these chemicals has caused an increase in skin cancer. Suggest a reason why.

_____ [1 mark]

B–A*

2 The graph shows the past, present and predicted future of the world human population.

a The human population is in the rapid growth stage. What is the name given to this stage of growth?

_____

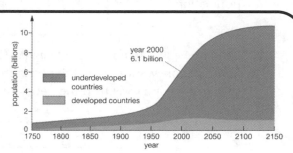

[1 mark]

b In developed countries, such as America, the population is constant. In underdeveloped countries, such as Africa, the population is still rising, yet underdeveloped countries cause less pollution. Suggest **two** reasons why.

1 _____

2 _____ [2 marks]

3 Scientists look for the water louse when they want to measure the level of pollution in water.

D–C

a Write down the name given to species that are used to measure levels of water pollution.

_____ [1 mark]

B–A*

b This table shows the sensitivity of different animals to pollution.

animal	sensitivity to pollution	animal	sensitivity to pollution
stonefly larva	sensitive	freshwater mussel	semi-sensitive
water snipe fly	sensitive	damselfly larva	semi-sensitive
alderfly	sensitive	bloodworm	tolerates pollution
mayfly larva	semi-sensitive	rat-tailed maggot	tolerates pollution

A river sample contains mussels, damselfly larva and bloodworms, but no alderfly or stonefly larva. Use this information to explain why the river sample is polluted.

_____

_____ [2 marks]

Sustainability

1 This is a picture of the dodo. The dodo no longer exists.
Suggest **two** reasons why the dodo no longer exists.

1 _____

2 _____ [2 marks]

2 Some animals are close to extinction. They are called **endangered species**.
The panda is an endangered species.

a Pandas are kept in captivity. Suggest how this may help increase the panda
population.

_____ [1 mark]

b Pandas live in a remote part of China. Their natural habitat is being destroyed.
Some people want to save the panda from extinction. Suggest **two** reasons why
saving the panda will help the people who live in the same habitat.

1 _____

2 _____ [2 marks]

3 a Some countries want to hunt whales for food. Suggest **one** argument for and
one argument against hunting whales.

For _____

_____

Against _____

_____ [2 marks]

b It is very difficult to stop people hunting whales.
Suggest **one** reason why.

_____ [1 mark]

4 a Sustainable resources are resources that should not run out. Fish are a sustainable
resource. The government has set fish quotas. Fishermen can only catch so many
fish at any one time. The fish quotas should help maintain the population of fish in
the sea. Explain why.

_____

_____ [2 marks]

b As the human population increases there will be more demand for energy
resources. The sustainable development of fast-growing willow trees could help
solve the problem. Explain why.

_____

_____ [2 marks]

D–C D–C B–A* D–C B–A* D–C B–A*

B2 Revision checklist

- I know how to collect and use data to estimate a population. ☐

- I know how to use a key to identify plants and animals. ☐

- I know the characteristics of the different vertebrate groups. ☐

- I can state the word and formula equation for photosynthesis. ☐

- I can describe the effect of increased light, temperature and carbon dioxide on photosynthesis rate. ☐

- I can explain how similar organisms compete for the same ecological niche. ☐

- I can explain how the size of a predator population will affect the prey population. ☐

- I can explain how adaptations of organisms determine their distribution and abundance. ☐

- I can explain how camels, polar bears and cacti are adapted to their habitats. ☐

- I can describe how organisms became fossilised. ☐

- I know that developed countries have a greater effect on world pollution. ☐

- I can explain the effects of increased pollution on climate change, acid rain and the ozone layer. ☐

- I can describe ways in which animals become extinct. ☐

- I can explain sustainable development and describe how it may protect endangered species. ☐

Molecules of life

1 Respiration is a chemical reaction that takes place in the cell.
Write down the name of the part of the cell where respiration takes place.

_____ [1 mark]

2 This diagram shows DNA fingerprints of individuals connected to a robbery.

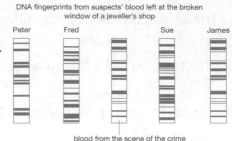

DNA fingerprints from suspects' blood left at the broken window of a jeweller's shop

Peter   Fred   Sue   James

blood from the scene of the crime

  a Who left blood at the crime scene? Explain your answer.

_____

_____

_____

_____

[2 marks]

  b Describe how a DNA fingerprint is made.

_____

_____

_____ [3 marks]

  c The DNA base code codes for amino acids.
    i How many amino acids are coded for in the following section of DNA?
    TATATGTAAAAACAA

_____ [1 mark]

    ii Write down the complementary base sequence for this section of DNA.

_____ [1 mark]

3 Look at the graph. It shows the effect of temperature on an enzyme.

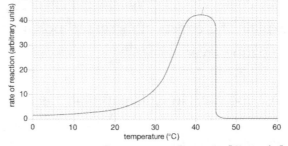

  a What is meant by the term **enzyme**?

_____

_____

_____

_____

[2 marks]

  b Describe the pattern shown in the graph.

_____

_____ [2 marks]

  c What is the optimum temperature of this enzyme?

_____ [1 mark]

  d The enzyme controlled reaction stops at 45 °C. Use ideas about enzyme shape to explain this.

_____

_____

_____ [3 marks]

Diffusion

D–C

1 a What is meant by the term **diffusion**?

_____

_____ [2 marks]

B–A*

b Diffusion takes place between cells of the body.
Describe **three** ways to increase the rate of diffusion between cells.

1 _____

2 _____

3 _____ [3 marks]

D–C

2 a Diffusion takes place in the placenta. Substances diffuse from the foetus into the mother's blood. Write down the name of **two** of these substances.

1 _____

2 _____ [2 marks]

b Diffusion of oxygen into the blood takes place in the lungs.
In which part of the lung does oxygen enter the blood?

_____ [1 mark]

D–C

3 Describe how carbon dioxide moves into the leaf. Use the words **concentration**, **diffusion** and **photosynthesis** in your answer.

_____

_____

_____ [3 marks]

B–A*

4 Look at the picture of a synapse. Describe how the synapse is adapted to carry the signal from one neurone to the next.

_____

_____

_____

_____

_____

_____ [3 marks]

Keep it moving

1 Red blood cells are adapted to carry out their function. They are disc-shaped and do not have a nucleus.

  a Explain how these adaptations allow them to support their function.

Disc-shaped _____

_____

No nucleus _____

_____ [2 marks]

  b Write down the name of the chemical that makes red blood cells red.

_____ [1 mark]

2 a Look at the diagram of the heart.

    i Draw an **X** to show the part of the heart that receives blood from the lungs.

    ii Label the bicuspid valve. [2 marks]

RIGHT   LEFT

  b The left ventricle has a thicker wall than the right ventricle. Explain why.

_____

_____ [2 marks]

  c People with heart disease may need a heart transplant.

    i Describe **two** problems with heart transplants.

1 _____

2 _____ [2 marks]

    ii Describe **one** advantage and **one** disadvantage that heart transplants have over heart pacemakers.

Advantage _____

Disadvantage _____ [2 marks]

3 a Describe the role of blood vessels in circulating blood around the body.

_____

_____

_____ [3 marks]

  b Humans have a double circulatory system. Explain the advantage of a double circulatory system.

_____

_____ [2 marks]

Divide and rule

D–C

1 a Amoebas are unicellular organisms. They only have one cell. Humans are multi-cellular; they are made of many cells. It may be a disadvantage to be unicellular rather than multi-cellular. Explain why.

_____

_____ [2 marks]

B–A*

b The table shows the surface area and volume of different cubes.
i Finish the table by calculating the surface area to volume ratio of each cube. The first one has been done for you.

cube	surface area in cm²	volume in cm³	ratio
A	24	8	24/8 = 3
B	54	27	
C	96	64	
D	150	125	

[3 marks]

ii Organisms made of a single large cell have a disadvantage. Use the information in the table to explain why.

_____

_____ [2 marks]

D–C

2 a Write down the name of the type of cell division that makes new **body** cells.

_____ [1 mark]

B–A*

b Which **two** of the following statements relate to the cell division that makes human body cells? Put ticks (✓) in the **two** correct boxes.

the new cells are diploid ☐

four new cells are made ☐

the new cells contain 23 chromosomes ☐

pairs of chromosomes separate to opposite poles of the cell ☐

the new cell shows variation ☐

chromosomes separate to opposite poles of the cell ☐ [2 marks]

D–C

3 a Sperm cells have a structure called an acrosome. Explain why sperm cells need an acrosome.

_____

_____ [2 marks]

B–A*

b A special type of cell division makes sperm cells.
i Write down the name of this type of cell division.

_____ [1 mark]

ii Describe **one** way in which this type of cell division is different from the cell division that makes body cells.

_____ [1 mark]

D–C

c Sperm cells are haploid. Explain is meant by the term **haploid**.

_____ [1 mark]

Growing up

1 a Both animal and plant cells have a nucleus which makes them similar.
Describe **one other** way that they are similar and **one** way they are different.

Similar _____

_____

Different _____

_____ [2 marks]

b For a fertilised egg to grow into an embryo the cells need to divide and change.

i Write down the name that is given to cells before they become specialised.

_____ [1 mark]

ii Damaged brain cells cause a disease called Parkinson's. Scientists hope to repair the damage by taking non-specialised cells from human embryos and then turning them into brain cells.
Explain why some people may object to this process.

_____

_____ [2 marks]

2 a Look at the table. It shows the change in weight of a baby aged from 0 to 30 months.

age in months	0	3	6	9	12	15	18	21	24	27	30
weight in kg	2.5	5.0	6.4	7.5	8.8	9.6	9.8	10.0	10.1	10.4	10.7

i Plot the points on the graph.

The first two have been done for you.

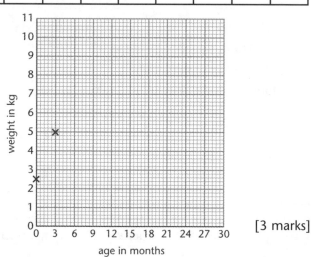

[3 marks]

ii Finish the graph by drawing the best curve. [1 mark]

iii Describe the pattern in the graph.

_____

_____ [2 marks]

iv Write down the phase of human growth shown in the graph.

_____ [1 mark]

b A baby should weigh about 14 kg at 30 months.
Suggest a reason why the baby represented in the graph is underweight.

_____ [1 mark]

Controlling plant growth

D–C

1 a Ben grows apple trees. He decides to take some shoot cuttings from his apple trees and uses rooting powder to grow new trees.
What effect does rooting powder have on the shoot cuttings?

_____ [1 mark]

b Ben also grows wheat and sprays the wheat with selective weedkiller.
The weedkiller destroys the weeds with broad leaves but not the crops.
i How does the weedkiller destroy the weeds?

_____

_____ [2 marks]

ii Explain why the crops are not affected by the weedkiller.

_____

_____ [2 marks]

2 a

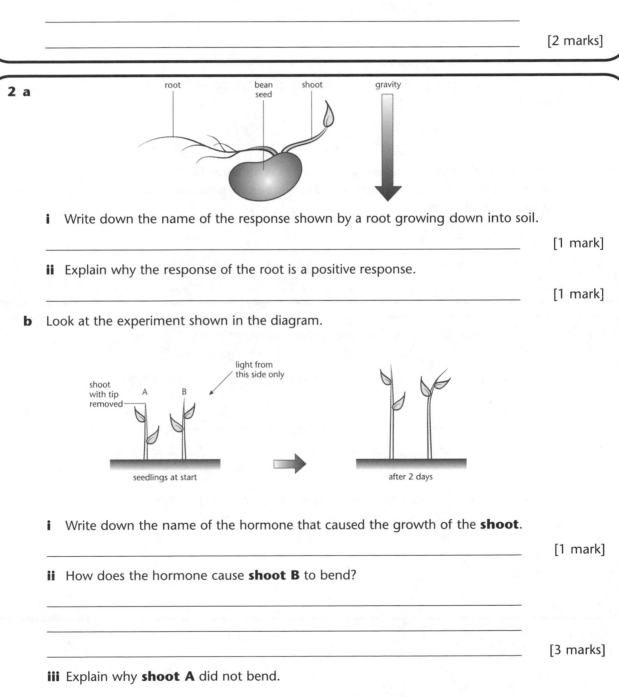

root   bean   shoot   gravity
         seed

i Write down the name of the response shown by a root growing down into soil.

_____ [1 mark]

ii Explain why the response of the root is a positive response.

_____ [1 mark]

D–C

B–A*

b Look at the experiment shown in the diagram.

light from this side only

shoot with tip removed   A   B

seedlings at start   after 2 days

i Write down the name of the hormone that caused the growth of the **shoot**.

_____ [1 mark]

ii How does the hormone cause **shoot B** to bend?

_____

_____

_____ [3 marks]

iii Explain why **shoot A** did not bend.

_____

_____ [2 marks]

New genes for old

1 Richard uses selective breeding to produce apples that are resistant to disease and green in colour. Describe the process of selective breeding.

_____

_____

_____   [3 marks]

2 When a gene mutates the base sequence changes. Look at the original base code and its mutation.

original base code	**AAAGGTCACTTGAAA**
mutation	**AAAGGTCACTGTAAA**

a Describe the mutation in this base code.

_____   [1 mark]

b Look at the flow chart. It shows how a white pigment is turned into a purple pigment using two enzymes.

                        enzyme A   enzyme B

white pigment ⟶ red pigment ⟶ purple pigment

The reactions take place in the petals of a flower. A mutation to the DNA resulted in red flowers. Use ideas about **base sequence**, **proteins** and **enzymes** to explain this.

_____

_____

_____   [3 marks]

3 Beta-carotene is needed to produce vitamin A. Beta-carotene is found in carrots but not in rice.

a Describe how genetic engineering can be used to grow rice that provides beta-carotene.

_____

_____

_____   [3 marks]

b Suggest **one** advantage and **one** disadvantage of genetic engineering.

Advantage _____

_____

Disadvantage _____

_____   [2 marks]

More of the same

1 a Describe how cows are cloned using **embryo transplants**.

_____

_____

_____ [3 marks]

b Scientists are hoping to solve organ transplant problems by cloning pigs.
  i Explain how the cloning of pigs could help solve organ transplant problems.

_____

_____ [2 marks]

  ii Suggest **one** reason why people may object to this process.

_____ [1 mark]

c Look at the diagram. It shows how Dolly the sheep was cloned.
  i Describe **two** ways in which nuclear transfer is different from embryo transplants.

egg cell taken from sheep A and nucleus removed

cells taken from the udder of sheep B and the nucleus removed

nucleus from sheep B is put into egg of sheep A

egg cell is put into a female sheep to grow

cell grows into a clone

1 _____

_____

_____

2 _____

_____

_____ [2 marks]

  ii The lamb produced is a clone of which sheep, A or B? Explain your answer.

_____ [1 mark]

2 Tissue culture can be used to clone plants.
  a Suggest **one** advantage and **one** disadvantage of cloning plants.

  Advantage _____

_____

  Disadvantage _____

_____ [2 marks]

  b Cloning plants is easier than cloning animals. Explain why.

_____

_____

_____ [3 marks]

B3 Revision checklist

- I can interpret data on DNA fingerprinting for identification. ☐

- I can describe DNA replication. ☐

- I know that food and oxygen diffuse across the placenta. ☐

- I can describe diffusion as the net movement of particles from a region of high concentration to a region of low concentration. ☐

- I can identify the main parts of the blood. ☐

- I can describe the roles of arteries, veins and capillaries. ☐

- I can label a diagram of the heart. ☐

- I know that a patient can reject a heart transplant. ☐

- I know that at fertilisation haploid gametes join to form a diploid zygote. ☐

- I know that body cells are made by mitosis and gametes are made by meiosis. ☐

- I can identify the main stages of human growth. ☐

- I know that shoots are positively phototropic and negatively geotropic; roots are the opposite. ☐

- I know that plant hormones affect plant growth and fruit ripening. ☐

- I know that changes to genes are called mutations. ☐

- I can describe the stages in selective breeding. ☐

- I know that genetic engineering is used to make insulin and improve crops. ☐

- I can describe some advantages and disadvantages of cloned plants. ☐

- I know that cloned animals could be used to produce organs for transplants. ☐

Who planted that there?

1 Look at the diagram. It shows the inside of a leaf.

D–C

  a Label

    i the upper epidermis

    ii a palisade cell

    iii a mesophyll cell

  b Put an **S** to show the
position of a stoma. [3 marks]

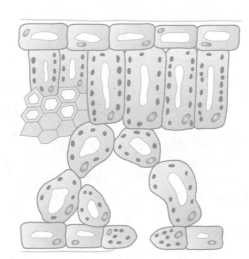

[1 mark]

2 Finish this sentence about gas exchange.

D–C

Carbon dioxide enters the leaf and oxygen leaves by _____ . [1 mark]

3 a A leaf is adapted for photosynthesis. It has broad leaves. This gives a large surface
area to absorb light. Write down **three other** ways they are adapted for photosynthesis.

D–C

  1 _____

  2 _____

  3 _____ [3 marks]

B–A*

  b The cells of a leaf are also adapted for maximum photosynthesis.
Explain how the cells are adapted.

    i Palisade cells _____

    _____

    _____ [2 marks]

    ii Mesophyll cells _____

    _____

    _____ [2 marks]

Water, water everywhere

1 a Lauren investigates osmosis. She put some potato chips into pure water and some into salt water. She left them for two hours. The diagram shows her results. Explain why the potato chip went floppy in salt water.

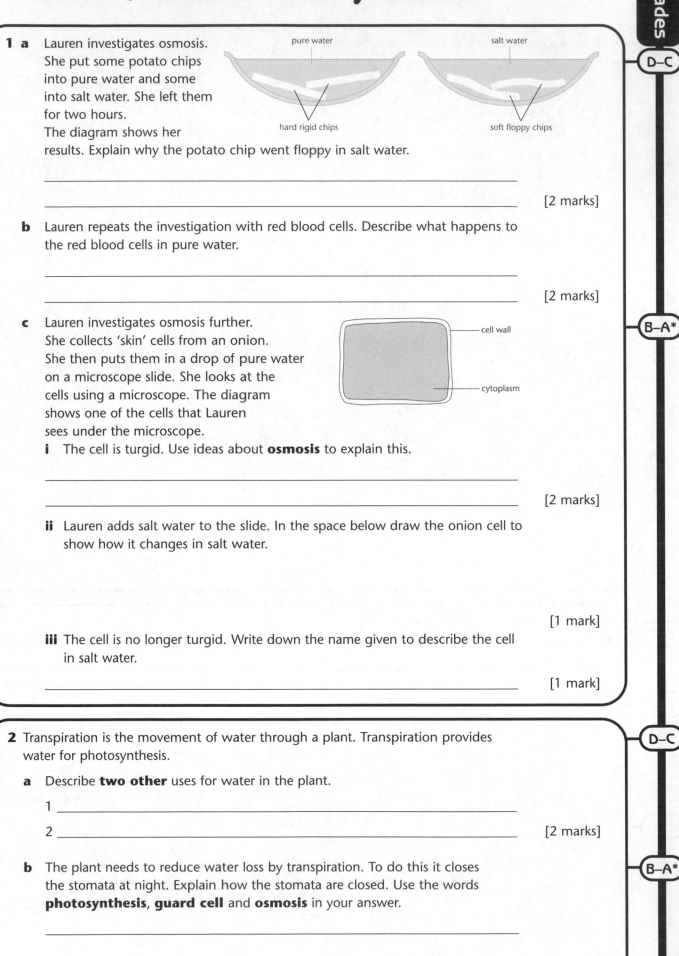

pure water salt water

hard rigid chips soft floppy chips

_____

_____ [2 marks]

b Lauren repeats the investigation with red blood cells. Describe what happens to the red blood cells in pure water.

_____

_____ [2 marks]

c Lauren investigates osmosis further. She collects 'skin' cells from an onion. She then puts them in a drop of pure water on a microscope slide. She looks at the cells using a microscope. The diagram shows one of the cells that Lauren sees under the microscope.

cell wall

cytoplasm

i The cell is turgid. Use ideas about **osmosis** to explain this.

_____

_____ [2 marks]

ii Lauren adds salt water to the slide. In the space below draw the onion cell to show how it changes in salt water.

[1 mark]

iii The cell is no longer turgid. Write down the name given to describe the cell in salt water.

_____ [1 mark]

2 Transpiration is the movement of water through a plant. Transpiration provides water for photosynthesis.

a Describe **two other** uses for water in the plant.

1 _____

2 _____ [2 marks]

b The plant needs to reduce water loss by transpiration. To do this it closes the stomata at night. Explain how the stomata are closed. Use the words **photosynthesis**, **guard cell** and **osmosis** in your answer.

_____

_____

_____ [3 marks]

Transport in plants

1 Look at the diagram. It shows the arrangement of cells in a cross section of a root.

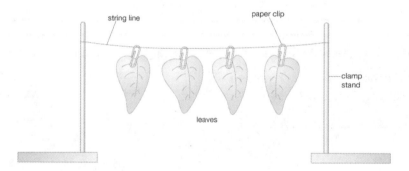

A   B

a Write down the names of the **two** types of cells shown in the diagram.

Cell **A** _____

Cell **B** _____

[2 marks]

b Describe the function of cell **B**.

_____

_____ [2 marks]

c Explain how the structure of **B** helps it carry out its function.

_____

_____ [2 marks]

2 Jasmine investigates transpiration in plants. She sets up two lines using this apparatus.

string line   paper clip

clamp
stand

leaves

a One line is kept in the dark and one line is kept in the light. The leaves in the **light** lost 7.4 g in mass. Suggest how much mass the leaves in the **dark** lost.

_____ [1 mark]

b Jasmine set up a third line and placed a clear plastic bag over the leaves.
  i Describe how this will affect the rate of transpiration.

_____ [1 mark]

  ii Explain how the plastic bag changed the rate of transpiration.

_____

_____ [2 marks]

Plants need minerals too

1 a Finish the table to show why a plant needs certain minerals.
The first one has been done for you.

mineral	why the mineral is needed	how the mineral is used
nitrate	*for cell growth*	*nitrogen is used to make amino acids*
phosphate		
potassium		
magnesium		

[6 marks]

b Mineral deficiency causes poor plant growth. A plant grown without nitrates will have poor growth and yellow leaves. Describe how a plant will look if it is grown without

i phosphate _____

_____ [2 marks]

ii potassium _____

_____ [2 marks]

iii magnesium _____

_____ [1 mark]

2 Look at the graph. It shows the uptake of minerals by algae living in pond water.

a What is the concentration of chlorine
   i in the cells of the algae?

_____

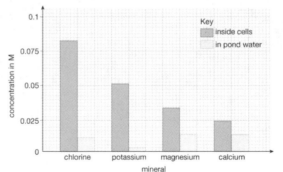

[1 mark]

ii in the pond water?

_____ [1 mark]

b Chlorine is not absorbed by diffusion. Explain why.

_____

_____ [2 marks]

c Name the type of transport that the algae use to take up chlorine from the pond water.

_____ [1 mark]

d Destroying the mitochondria inside the algae stops the uptake of minerals. Explain why.

_____

_____ [2 marks]

Energy flow

D–C

1 Look at the diagram. It shows a pyramid of numbers.

10s of foxes

100s of shrews

1000s of caterpillars

oak tree

  a Explain what information is shown in a pyramid of numbers.

  _____

  _____

  _____   [2 marks]

  b In the space below draw a pyramid of biomass for the same food chain.

                                                                         [1 mark]

  c As energy flows through the food chain some is lost. Write down **one** way in
  which energy is lost.

  _____   [1 mark]

B–A*

2 Farmers who grow crops produce large amounts of biomass. The biomass has
many uses. They may choose to eat the biomass or feed it to their cows.

  a Suggest **two other** ways they may choose to use the biomass.

  1 _____

  2 _____   [2 marks]

  b Look at the diagram. It shows the energy transfer from
  the farmer's crops to the cow.

    i Calculate the amount of energy used for growth.

      Energy used for growth _____kJ   [2 marks]

    ii Calculate the efficiency of energy transfer of the cow.

      Energy efficiency _____%   [2 marks]

  1022 kJ in heat loss

  Sun

  energy for growth

  1909 kJ in waste

  3090 kJ energy in 1 m² of crops

  c Some people think it is better to grow crops for food
  instead of producing meat to eat.
  Use your answer to part **b** to explain why.

  _____   [1 mark]

D–C

3 a Brazil produces a lot of sugar cane. The sugar cane is used to produce a biofuel.
  Describe how. Use the words **yeast**, **fermentation** and **petrol** in your answer.

  _____

  _____

  _____   [3 marks]

B–A*

  b Describe **one** advantage and **one** disadvantage of using biofuels.

  Advantage _____

  _____   [1 mark]

  Disadvantage _____

  _____   [1 mark]

Farming

1 a DDT is a chemical that can be used to kill insects.
Look at the food chain from a marine environment.
plankton ⟶ krill ⟶ penguin ⟶ seal
DDT contaminated the water. The plankton absorbed the DDT but did not die.
The seals began to die from the DDT.
Explain why.

_____

_____

_____ [3 marks]

D–C

b Look at the picture. It shows intensive farming of pigs.
This type of farming is more energy efficient than keeping
pigs outside. Explain why.

_____

_____

_____ [2 marks]

B–A*

2 a Describe how tomatoes can be grown without soil.

_____

_____ [2 marks]

D–C

b Write down **one** advantage and **one** disadvantage of growing tomatoes without soil.

Advantage _____

_____

Disadvantage _____

_____ [2 marks]

B–A*

3 a Organic farmers use a method of farming called crop rotation to help the soil.
Describe **two other** methods of farming used by organic farmers.

1 _____ [1 mark]

2 _____ [1 mark]

D–C

b Organic farming is not possible in countries such as Ethiopia.
Suggest why.

_____

_____ [2 marks]

B–A*

c In 1935 large cane toads were introduced into Australia to control insects feeding on sugar
cane. The toads did not eat the insects; they ate native toads instead. The cane toads have
no predators in Australia.
i Write down the name given to this type of pest control.

_____ [1 mark]

ii The cane toads are now bigger pests than the insects they were sent to control.
Suggest **one** reason why.

_____ [1 mark]

D–C

Decay

1 a Look at the apparatus Shahid
uses to investigate decay.
Both samples are weighed, left
for two days and then re-weighed.

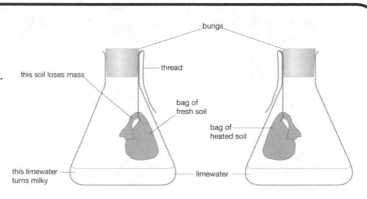

bungs

thread

this soil loses mass

bag of
fresh soil

bag of
heated soil

this limewater
turns milky

limewater

The table shows Shahid's results.

mass in g	bag of fresh soil	bag of heated soil
at start	6.2	6.5
at end	5.8	6.5
change		0

i Calculate the change in mass of the bag of fresh soil.
Write your answer in the shaded box.

[1 mark]

ii The heated soil did not change in mass. Explain why.

_____

_____ [2 marks]

b Earthworms feed on the remains of dead and decaying organisms.
How do earthworms help microorganisms to increase the rate of decay?

_____

_____ [2 marks]

c Shahid extends the investigation. He sets up four more bags of fresh soil and
leaves them at different temperatures.
i Predict which of Shahid's bags lost the most mass. Put a (ring) around
the correct answer.

bag A 10 °C   **bag B 20 °C**   **bag C 40 °C**   **bag D 60 °C** [1 mark]

ii Explain your answer to part **c i**.

_____

_____ [2 marks]

d Fungi such as mushrooms are called saprophytes. Describe how fungi feed on
dead plant material.

_____

_____ [2 marks]

2 Jennifer grows strawberries but she has too many to eat before they decay.
She preserves the strawberries by making jam.
Explain how this method slows down the decay of the strawberries.

_____

_____ [2 marks]

Recycling

1 The diagram shows the carbon cycle.

a Finish labelling the carbon cycle. Choose **three** words from this list.

burning
digestion
feeding
photosynthesis
reproduction
respiration

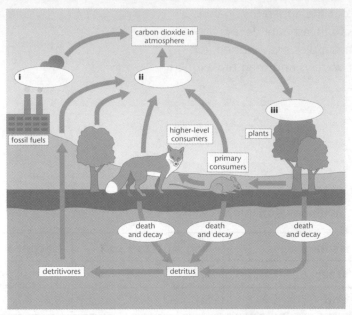

[3 marks]

b Write down the name of the process that removes carbon dioxide from the air.

_____ [1 mark]

c Decomposers return carbon dioxide to the air. Explain why.

_____
_____ [2 marks]

d Look at the picture. It shows marine animals called corals. The carbon in the shells of coral is recycled over millions of years. Explain how this occurs.

_____
_____
_____
_____ [3 marks]

2 In the nitrogen cycle, plants take up nitrates from the soil.

a Why do plants need nitrates?

_____ [1 mark]

b The nitrates are returned to the soil by decomposers. Explain how.

_____
_____ [2 marks]

c Nitrogen gas in the air cannot be used directly by plants. Explain why.

_____ [1 mark]

d Describe **two** ways nitrogen gas can be turned into nitrates for the plants.

1 _____

2 _____ [2 marks]

e Write down the name of the bacteria that return nitrogen to the air.

_____ [1 mark]

B4 Revision checklist

- I can label a diagram showing the parts of a leaf. ☐

- I can explain how a leaf is adapted for photosynthesis. ☐

- I know that osmosis is the movement of water molecules across a partially-permeable membrane. ☐

- I can describe the structure of xylem and phloem. ☐

- I can explain how transpiration rate can be increased. ☐

- I know that active transport needs energy from respiration. ☐

- I can identify mineral deficiencies in plants. ☐

- I can construct pyramids of numbers and biomass. ☐

- I can explain the reasons for developing biofuels. ☐

- I can describe the difference between intensive farming and organic farming. ☐

- I know that a saprophyte decays organisms by releasing enzymes. ☐

- I can explain why the different preservation methods stop food decay. ☐

- I can describe the carbon cycle. ☐

- I can describe the nitrogen cycle. ☐

In good shape

1 This question is about skeletons.

a One advantage the human skeleton has compared to the insect skeleton is flexibility.

Write down **two other** advantages.

1 _____

2 _____ [2 marks]

b Read the statements about human long bones.

Put a tick (✓) in the box next to the correct statement.

the shaft is made of cartilage ☐

the shaft is made of solid bone ☐

the shaft is empty ☐

the shaft contains bone marrow ☐ [1 mark]

c Describe the process of ossification.

_____

_____ [2 marks]

2 Bones can be broken in different ways.

a Explain why old people are more likely to break their bones.

_____ [1 mark]

b The muscles of the arm pull the arm in different directions by relaxing and contracting.

What term is used to describe muscles that work together in this way?

_____ muscles [1 mark]

c Hip joints contain a fluid.

i Write down the name used to describe this fluid.

_____ [1 mark]

ii Describe the job of this fluid.

_____

_____ [2 marks]

d Artificial hip replacements are now common operations.

Describe **one** advantage and **one** disadvantage of artificial hip replacements.

Advantage _____

Disadvantage _____ [2 marks]

The vital pump

Grades

1 This question is about the heart.

D–C

a There are four main blood vessels attached to the heart.

Write down the name of the vessel that takes blood:

i away from the **left** ventricle

_____ [1 mark]

ii away from the **right** ventricle

_____ [1 mark]

B–A*

b Describe the cardiac cycle of the human heart. Start with blood entering the atrium.

In your answer include ideas about:

– diastole

– systole

– contraction and relaxation of the different chambers.

_____

_____

_____ [3 marks]

2 a Special cells in the heart control the heartbeat.

D–C

i Write down the name that describes these cells.

_____ [1 mark]

B–A*

ii Describe how these cells coordinate heart muscle contraction.

_____

_____

_____ [3 marks]

D–C

b Doctors use different machines to check the heart.

Which machine is used to:

i record nerve impulses to the heart?

_____ [1 mark]

ii produce pictures of a working heart?

_____ [1 mark]

B–A*

c Look at the graph. It shows changes in electrical impulses in the heart.

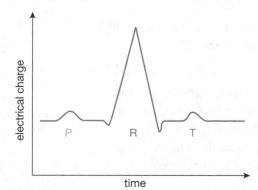

Which letter represents contraction of the ventricles: P, R or T? _____ [1 mark]

Running repairs

1 There are many different heart conditions.

a Finish the sentences about heart conditions.

At birth, a hole can be left between the left and right side of the heart. This 'hole in the heart' means blood leaving the heart carries less _____.

The coronary artery can become _____. This can result in a heart attack.

Doctors have found that '**heart-assist**' devices can reduce the work done by

heart _____.

The valves in the heart may become damaged. This causes some blood to flow

back into the atria reducing blood _____. [4 marks]

b Many factors of modern life can contribute to a poor circulatory system.

One factor is a fatty diet.

Write about **other** factors.

_____

_____

_____ [3 marks]

c Write down the name of the pigment found in red blood cells.

_____ [1 mark]

d Describe how a white blood cell is adapted to destroy bacteria.

_____ [1 mark]

2 Read the statements about blood clotting.

Put ticks (✓) in the boxes next to the **two** correct statements.

Someone with haemophilia can easily clot his or her blood. ☐

Haemophilia is an inherited condition. ☐

Vitamin C can affect clotting. ☐

Making cranberries part of your diet will help with blood clotting. ☐

Warfarin is a chemical used to help the blood clot. ☐ [2 marks]

3 Look at the diagram. It shows the different blood groups.

a Which group of people are called 'universal donors'?

_____ [1 mark]

b People with group AB can only donate their blood to a person with AB blood.
Use ideas about antigens and antibodies to explain why.

Blood group		Can donate to:	Can receive from:
A	A antigen / B antibody	AB	O
B	B antigen / A antibody	AB	O
AB	B antigen / A antigen	same group only	O
O	B antibody / A antibody	A, B or AB	same group only

_____

_____ [2 marks]

Breath of life

Grades

D–C

1 A spirometer can be used to measure breathing rate.

  a The diagram shows a spirometer trace for a student.

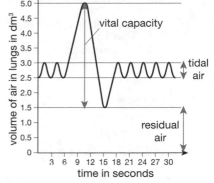

   i What is meant by the term **residual air**?

   _____ [1 mark]

   ii What is the **vital capacity** of this student?

   _____ dm³ [1 mark]

B–A*

   iii The breathing rate is shown by the number of complete waves (crest to crest) in a minute.

   Calculate the breathing rate of this student between 18 and 30 seconds.

   You are advised to show your working.

   _____ breaths per minute   [3 marks]

  b The lungs are adapted for efficient diffusion of oxygen into the blood.

   One adaptation is their large surface area.

   Describe **two other** adaptations.

   1 _____

   2 _____   [2 marks]

---

2 Asthma is one disease of the respiratory system.

D–C

  a Describe **one** symptom and **one** treatment of an asthma attack.

   Symptom _____

   Treatment _____   [2 marks]

B–A*

  b Look at the graph. It shows incidences of respiratory diseases.

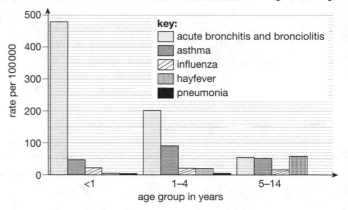

   i Which age group is more likely to suffer from asthma?

   _____ [1 mark]

   ii Only one respiratory disease becomes more common from age 0 to 14.

   Which one?

   _____ [1 mark]

D–C

3 The lining of the trachea is covered by millions of tiny hair-like structures.

  a What name is used to describe these structures?

   _____ [1 mark]

  b The hair-like structures help protect the respiratory system from disease.

   Describe how the respiratory system protects itself from disease.

   _____

   _____   [2 marks]

Waste disposal

1 This question is about excretion.

   a The kidney filters the blood and makes urine.

      i Write down the name of the blood vessel that takes blood into the kidney.

      _____ [1 mark]

      ii Write down the name of the tube that takes urine from the kidney to the bladder.

      _____ [1 mark]

   b Look at the diagram of a kidney tubule.

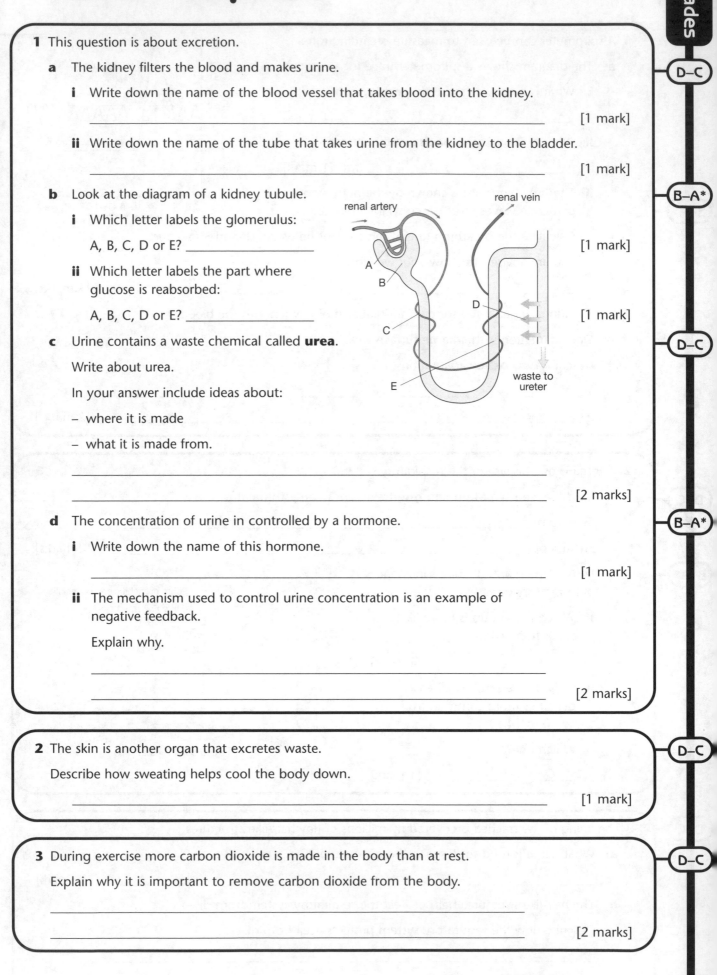

      i Which letter labels the glomerulus:

      A, B, C, D or E? _____ [1 mark]

      ii Which letter labels the part where glucose is reabsorbed:

      A, B, C, D or E? _____ [1 mark]

   c Urine contains a waste chemical called **urea**.

     Write about urea.

     In your answer include ideas about:

     – where it is made

     – what it is made from.

     _____

     _____ [2 marks]

   d The concentration of urine in controlled by a hormone.

      i Write down the name of this hormone.

      _____ [1 mark]

      ii The mechanism used to control urine concentration is an example of negative feedback.

        Explain why.

      _____

      _____ [2 marks]

2 The skin is another organ that excretes waste.

   Describe how sweating helps cool the body down.

   _____ [1 mark]

3 During exercise more carbon dioxide is made in the body than at rest.

   Explain why it is important to remove carbon dioxide from the body.

   _____

   _____ [2 marks]

Life goes on

1 a Write about the menstrual cycle.

In your answer include ideas about:

– menstruation

– ovulation

– thickness of the uterus lining.

_____

_____

_____ [3 marks]

b Hormones control the menstrual cycle.

Describe the job of these hormones in controlling the menstrual cycle.

FSH _____

LH _____

Progesterone _____ [3 marks]

2 IVF is one treatment for infertility.

a Describe the main stages in IVF treatment.

_____

_____ [2 marks]

b Describe **one** advantage and **one** disadvantage of infertility treatment.

Advantage _____

Disadvantage _____ [2 marks]

c A pregnant mother is concerned that her baby could have Down's syndrome.

The doctors take a sample of the fluid from around the baby in the uterus.

i Write down the name given to this process of taking fluid.

_____ [1 mark]

ii Describe how the doctors take the fluid.

_____

_____ [2 marks]

d The result of the test indicates that the baby may have Down's syndrome.

The parents decide to continue the pregnancy.

Write about **two** of the issues the parents need to consider

1 _____

2 _____ [2 marks]

New for old

1 Mechanical replacements can be used as transplants to replace some parts of the body.

a A mechanical transplant cannot replace the kidney.

However a machine can replace the kidney outside the body.

Write down the term used to describe this machine.

_____ [1 mark]

b The kidney machine is too big to fit inside the body.

Size is one problem of using mechanical replacements.

Write down **two other** problems.

1 _____

2 _____ [2 marks]

c Kidney transplants have been available under the NHS since the 1960s.

The success rate of kidney transplants has improved since then.

Suggest one reason why.

_____ [1 mark]

2 a Look at the table.

It shows the number of people waiting for transplants in the UK in January 2006.

kidney	liver	lungs	heart	pancreas	heart & lungs
5706	334	258	97	51	40

Write down **two** reasons why the waiting list is so long.

1 _____

2 _____ [2 marks]

b The body can reject organ transplants.

Write about how doctors can reduce the chance of rejection.

_____

_____ [2 marks]

c In the UK, people have to register to become organ donors.

It has been suggested that everyone becomes a donor unless they opt out of the system.

Write down **one** reason for and **one** against an 'opt out' system of organ donation.

Reason for _____

Reason against _____ [2 marks]

Size matters

1 This question is about growth.

Look at the growth chart for a boy age 1 to 5 years old.

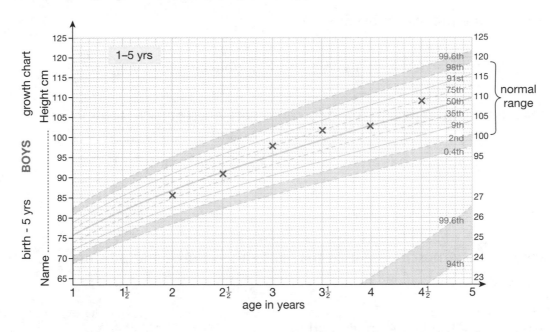

a Write down the height of the boy at age 3 years. _____cm   [1 mark]

b Calculate the change in height between the age of 3 and 4 years.

You are advised to show your working. _____cm   [2 marks]

2 a Life expectancy has changed in recent years.

   i Describe how it has changed.

   _____   [1 mark]

   ii Suggest **two** reasons for this change.

    1 _____

    2 _____   [2 marks]

b The change in life expectancy can cause problems on a personal and national level.

Write about some of these problems.

Personal problems _____

_____

National problems _____

_____   [3 marks]

3 The human growth hormone controls growth.

   a Write down the name of the organ that makes human growth hormone.

   _____   [1 mark]

   b Describe the effect of human growth hormone on the liver.

   _____   [1 mark]

B5 Revision checklist

- I can describe the advantages of an internal skeleton. ☐

- I can describe the process of ossification. ☐

- I know the difference between a single and a double circulatory system. ☐

- I can describe how the pacemaker cells coordinate heart muscle contraction. ☐

- I can discuss the advantages and disadvantages of heart transplants. ☐

- I can interpret data on heart disease. ☐

- I can describe how muscles are used to change the volume and pressure inside the chest. ☐

- I can explain how the kidney makes urine. ☐

- I can describe different treatments of infertility. ☐

- I know how the hormones control the menstrual cycle. ☐

- I know why there is a shortage of organ donors. ☐

- I can discuss the ethical issues concerning organ transplants. ☐

- I can describe how diet and exercise can influence growth. ☐

- I know where human growth hormone is made in the body. ☐

Understanding bacteria

D–C

1 Bacteria can be classified by their shape. Round bacteria are called spherical.

a Write down the names of **two other** bacteria shapes.

1 _____

2 _____ [2 marks]

b Bacteria reproduce asexually by splitting in half.

i Write down the name of this type of special asexual reproduction.

_____ [1 mark]

ii Bacteria that get inside our bodies reproduce very quickly.

Suggest why this is a problem.

_____ [1 mark]

B–A*

c Some bacteria can use ammonia to make proteins.

Which element in the ammonia is essential for protein synthesis?

_____ [1 mark]

D–C

2 a Karen makes some yoghurt

i Here are four sentences (**A–D**) about how she makes some yoghurt.

They are in the wrong order.

Fill in the boxes to show the correct order.

The first one has been done for you.

A Bacteria is added to the milk and left at 46 °C for 4 hours.

B Milk is heated to 95 °C then cooled.

C The yoghurt is cooled and packed.

D Flavours are added.

B			

[2 marks]

ii Karen has to use sterilised equipment. Explain why.

_____ [1 mark]

B–A*

b Bacteria can be grown on an agar dish.

i Disposable gloves are worn while handling bacteria.

Explain why.

_____

_____ [1 mark]

ii It is important that the lids are not left off the dishes.

Explain why.

_____ [1 mark]

Harmful microorganisms

1 a Write down the term used to describe a microorganism that causes disease.

_____ [1 mark]

D–C

b After infection by a microorganism, it takes time for the symptoms to appear.

During this time the microorganisms are reproducing.

Write down the term used to describe the time between infection and the appearance of symptoms.

_____ [1 mark]

c Look at the graph. It shows the number of cholera cases between 1993 and 2003.

B–A*

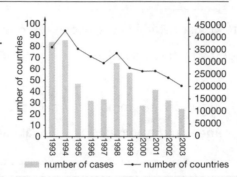

i In which year were the lowest number of cases reported?

_____ [1 mark]

ii Describe the link between the number of countries reporting cases and the number of cases reported.

_____ [1 mark]

iii What was unusual about 1997 compared to 1996?

_____ [1 mark]

2 a Penicillin can be used to cure bacterial infection.

D–C

i Write down the name of the scientist who discovered penicillin.

_____ [1 mark]

ii Penicillin is a type of microorganism. Which type?

_____ [1 mark]

b Joseph Lister made an important discovery about the treatment of diseases.

Describe Joseph Lister's discovery.

_____

_____ [2 marks]

c Diseases can spread quickly after a natural disaster such as an earthquake.

Aid organisations in a disaster area view clean water as a top priority.

i Which **two** diseases can spread if there is no clean water?

1 _____

2 _____ [2 marks]

ii Damage to electrical supplies can also lead to the spread of disease.

B–A*

Explain why.

_____ [1 mark]

D–C

Microorganisms – factories for the future?

1 a One condition needed for the optimum growth of yeast is the correct temperature.

Write down **two other** conditions needed for optimum growth.

1 _____

2 _____ [2 marks]

b Water is used to clean the equipment used in food production. The water can become contaminated with sugar. Yeast can be used to clean the water.

Explain why.

_____ [1 mark]

c To produce alcohol, yeast must be grown without oxygen.

Explain why.

_____

_____ [2 marks]

2 a During the process of making beer, the beer is clarified and pasteurised.

i What is meant by the term **clarified**?

_____ [1 mark]

ii Why is it important to pasteurise the beer?

_____ [1 mark]

b The alcohol content of a drink can be increases by the process of distillation.

Describe the process of distillation.

_____

_____ [2 marks]

c Look at the graph. It shows the growth of two different strains of yeast over time.

i Which strain shows a higher tolerance for alcohol? Explain your answer.

Strain _____

Reason _____ [2 marks]

ii A higher tolerance for alcohol is one reason for using a different strain of yeast to make alcohol.

Write down **one other** reason why different strains are used.

_____ [1 mark]

iii Louis Pasteur was very important to the wine industry.

Explain why.

_____

_____ [2 marks]

Biofuels

1 Look at the picture of a digester.

The digester is used to make biogas.

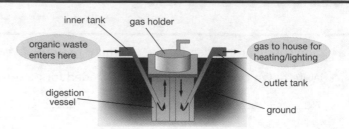

a The digester can make biogas without stopping for several years.

What term describes this method of making something without stopping for a long time?

_____ [1 mark]

b The graph shows the effect of temperature on the volume of biogas produced.

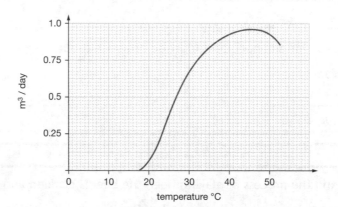

i Describe the pattern in the graph.

_____

_____ [2 marks]

ii Use ideas about enzymes to explain the pattern in the graph.

_____

_____ [3 marks]

c Finish the diagram to show the products of bacterial action on plant and animals waste.

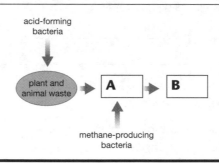

[2 marks]

---

2 Biofuels such as gasohol have advantages over fossil fuels.

a One advantage is that they are renewable energy sources.

Describe **two other** advantages.

1 _____

2 _____ [2 marks]

b Palm oil can be used as a biofuel. Large areas of rainforest are cut down and burnt to grow palm oil plants. Some people object to this.

Suggest **two** reasons why.

1 _____

2 _____ [2 marks]

Life in soil

1 a Earthworms live in soil. They burrow through the soil. This makes the soil better for growing plants.

Explain why.

_____

_____

_____ [3 marks]

b Charles Darwin realised that few plants would grow in soil without earthworms.

Write about his ideas to explain the importance of earthworms.

_____

_____ [2 marks]

c Waterlogged soil can be improved by adding sand.

Explain why adding the sand helps more plants to grow.

_____

_____

_____ [3 marks]

2 a Bacteria in the soil recycle different elements such as nitrogen.

Why is it important that these elements are recycled?

_____ [1 mark]

b Look at the diagram of a food web.

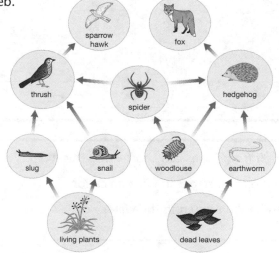

Use the food web to answer these questions.

i Write down the name of **one** herbivore.

_____ [1 mark]

ii Write down the name of **one** detritivore.

_____ [1 mark]

iii Write down the name of **one** carnivore.

_____ [1 mark]

c Describe the role of nitrifying bacteria in the nitrogen cycle.

_____

_____ [2 marks]

Microscopic life in water

1 Adult frogs develop from young called tadpoles. Tadpoles live in water.

a There are advantages and disadvantages to living in water.

Write down **one** advantage and **one** disadvantage.

Advantage _____

Disadvantage _____ [2 marks]

b The life cycle of a frog reduces the competition between adults and young.

Describe **one** reason why.

_____ [1 mark]

c *Amoeba* are microscopic animals that live in fresh water. The water they live in is more dilute than their cytoplasm.

i Explain why this is a problem.

_____

_____ [2 marks]

ii Describe the process *Amoeba* use to solve the problem.

You may use labelled diagrams in your answer.

_____

_____ [2 marks]

2 Fertiliser run-off from farms can cause eutrophication.

a Describe the main stages in eutrophication.

Start with fertiliser entering the water.

_____

_____

_____ [3 marks]

b Pesticide from farms can also enter the water causing problems to wildlife.

Explain why pesticides are a problem.

Use ideas about **food chains** in your answer.

_____

_____

_____ [3 marks]

D–C

B–A*

D–C

B–A*

Enzymes in action

1 Different enzymes used in washing powders digest different types of stains.

a The list shows some different enzymes.

Draw a **straight** line from the enzyme to one type of stain that it removes.

enzyme	stain
amylase	starch
lipase	protein
protease	fat

[2 marks]

b Sucrase is an enzyme used to breakdown sucrose.

i Explain why this enzyme is useful to the food industry.

_____ [1 mark]

ii Finish the word equation to show the action of sucrase.

sucrase

sucrose ⟶ _____ + _____ [2 marks]

2 Enzymes can be immobilised by covering them in alginate.

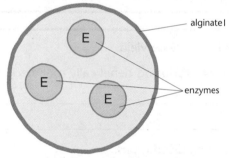

alginate

E

E

E

enzymes

a Describe **two** advantages of immobilising enzymes.

1 _____

2 _____ [2 marks]

b Immobilised enzymes can be used to make lactose-free milk.

Write down the name of the enzyme used to make lactose-free milk.

_____ [1 mark]

c Lactose-free milk is often produced for cats.

i Explain why cats need lactose-free milk.

_____ [1 mark]

ii Describe what happens in a cat's digestive system if they drink milk containing lactose.

_____

_____ [2 marks]

Genetic engineering

1 Scientists can change the DNA of an organism.

a Write down the term that describes an organism that has had its DNA changed.

_____   [1 mark]

b The process of changing the DNA of an organism involves several stages.

First a section of DNA (a gene) is removed from one organism.

   i Describe the next **two** stages.

     1 _____

     2 _____   [2 marks]

   ii Which type of enzyme is needed to remove the DNA from the organism?

     _____ enzyme   [1 mark]

c Assaying techniques are used to check that the DNA has gone into the new organism.

Describe how scientists check that human DNA has stuck in the DNA of bacteria.

_____

_____

_____   [3 marks]

D–C
B–A*

2 Crops are often genetically modified to increase yield.

a Write down **two other** reasons for producing genetically modified crops.

     1 _____

     2 _____   [2 marks]

b Some people object to genetically modified crops.

Suggest **two** reasons why.

     1 _____

     2 _____   [2 marks]

D–C
B–A*

3 Human insulin can now be made using bacteria.

Describe how this is done.

In your answer use ideas about:

– human DNA

– plasmids

– cloning.

_____

_____

_____   [3 marks]

D–C

B6 Revision checklist

- I know the functions of each part of the bacterial cell. ☐

- I can explain why bacteria are able to exploit a wide range of habitats. ☐

- I know about the work of Pasteur, Lister and Fleming. ☐

- I can describe how natural disasters cause a rapid spread of diseases. ☐

- I can describe the main stages in brewing beer and wine. ☐

- I can describe how methane is made. ☐

- I can describe the importance of earthworms to soil structure and fertility. ☐

- I can explain the part played by bacteria in the nitrogen cycle. ☐

- I can describe the advantages and disadvantages of living in water. ☐

- I can explain how animals cope with the problems of living in fresh water and salt water. ☐

- I can describe the advantages of immobilised enzymes. ☐

- I know different examples of immobilised enzymes and the chemicals that they break down. ☐

- I can describe the main stages in genetic engineering. ☐

- I can discuss the advantages and disadvantages of genetic engineering. ☐

Glossary

A

A,T,C,G The four bases found in DNA, adenine, thymine, cytosine and guanine.

acetylcholine Chemical that carries signals across the tiny gaps between nerve cells.

acrosome A bubble of enzymes at the front of a sperm.

active immunity When the body has made antibodies so it can recognise a pathogen if it invades the body a second time.

active transport When cells use energy to transport substances through cell membranes against a concentration gradient.

adaptation A feature that helps an organism survive, e.g. polar bears have thick fur to keep warm.

aerobic respiration Breakdown of glucose using oxygen to make energy available for chemical reactions in cells.

allele Different form of a gene. Inherited features are carried as pairs of alleles on a pair of chromosomes. A feature may be the result of a single gene acting or may involve several genes working together.

alveoli The sac-like end of an airway in the lungs; the surface is enlarged to maximise gas exchange.

amino acid The sub-units making up protein molecules; there are over 20 different amino acids used by living things.

amniocentesis Taking a sample of cells from the fluid that surrounds a foetus.

amphibian An animal that spends some of its life cycle in water and some on land.

anaerobic respiration A series of chemical reactions that transfer energy from glucose into life processes without using oxygen.

antagonistic muscle Two muscles that pull in opposite directions.

antibody Chemicals produced by cells called b lymphocytes which attack invading microorganisms.

anti-coagulant Chemical used to stop the blood clotting.

antigen Chemicals found in cell membranes which trigger a reaction by the immune system.

artery Blood vessel carrying blood away from the heart under high pressure.

aseptic technique Technique used in microbiological work to prevent infection or contamination of cultures.

asexual reproduction Reproduction involving just one parent; the offspring are genetically identical to the parent.

atrium A thin-walled chamber in the heart, above the ventricle.

auxin Chemical produced by the growing tips of plants that promotes cell growth and elongation.

B

bacteria Microscopic, single-celled living things that have no nucleus.

base sequence The sequence of bases on a molecule of DNA.

benign A tumour is benign if the cells are contained and have not invaded other tissues. Benign tumours do not stimulate the growth of tumours in other parts of the body.

binary fission Form of asexual reproduction that involves splitting the parent into two daughter cells, e.g. budding in yeast.

binocular Something with two eyepieces or two eyes, e.g. binocular vision uses two eyes to judge distances.

biodiversity The range of different organisms in an area.

biofuel Fuel that is produced by a living organism, e.g. wood or oil from a plant like rapeseed.

biogas Mixture of gases made when waste is digested by microorganisms which burns to release energy.

biological control Release of a natural predator to reduce the number of pests infesting a crop.

biological washing powder Contains enzymes to digest grease and protein stains.

biomass The mass of living material in an area.

blood groups A way of sorting blood into different types depending on the immunity proteins it contains; there are four common blood groups, A, B, AB and O.

blood pressure The pressure of blood in your arteries and veins.

blood transfusion Transferring blood obtained from one person into another through a needle or tube.

BMI A calculation used to find out if you are the correct weight for your height.

C

camouflage When an organisms blends into the background because of its colour.

capillary The narrowest type of blood vessel; red blood cells can only pass through it in single file.

carbohydrase Enzyme that can digest carbohydrates.

carnivore Animal that eats other animals.

cell differentiation The change of an unspecialised cell into a particular type of cell.

cell division The multiplication of cells.

cell wall A thick wall consisting of cellulose found around plant cells.

cellulose An insoluble carbohydrate molecule formed from spirals of glucose joined together; cell walls in plants are made of cellulose.

central nervous system The brain and spinal cord.

characteristic Things that are true about something, e.g. it is a characteristic of mammals that they have fur.

chlorophyll A green chemical found in photosynthetic plants that allows them to use energy from sunlight to make sugar from carbon dioxide and water.

chloroplast A cell structure found in green plants that contains chlorophyll.

cholesterol Chemical found particularly in animal fats and foods made from them; the body uses cholesterol to make nerve tissue and some hormones, but high levels of cholesterol may make heart attacks more likely.

chromosome A thread-like body made of DNA and protein found in the nucleus, it only becomes visible during cell division.

cilia Tiny hairs found on the surface of cells and some microorganisms. Cilia in the lungs wave in patterns to move liquids over the surface of the cells. Some bacteria are covered in cilia which wave to move the bacteria along.

cirrhosis A disease of the liver often caused by excessive alcohol intake. Cirrhotic livers have a lot of fibrous tissues and cannot break down toxins as well as healthy livers.

clone Two living things are clones if they have exactly the same genes.

community All the different species living in the same ecosystem.

compost Organic material, typically kitchen and garden waste, being rotted down to make fertiliser for the soil.

consumer Organisms in an ecosystem that use up organic matter produced by other organisms; all animals are consumers.

coronary artery The artery that supplies blood to the muscles of the heart.

crenation Process in which cells become partly deflated and have a scalloped edge because they have shrunk, e.g. when red blood cells shrink in concentrated solutions.

cuticle The waxy outer layer of the skin or the surface of a leaf.

cyclic fluctuation Populations which rise and fall regularly, e.g. the numbers of predators and their prey.

D

Darwin Charles Darwin was the Victorian biologist who put forward the theory of evolution in his book *The origin of species*.

decay To rot.

decomposer An organism that breaks down dead organic matter.

denatured A molecule that has had its shape altered so that it cannot do its job efficiently, e.g. proteins denatured by heat.

denitrifying bacteria Bacteria that break down complex nitrogenous substances and release nitrogen gas.

deoxyribonucleic acid The molecule that carries the genetic information in animals and higher plants; abbreviated to DNA.

detritivore An organism that eats dead and decaying organic matter.

detritus The dead and semi-decayed remains of living things.

diabetes A disease caused by the failure to control levels of sugar in the blood because the pancreas cannot secrete insulin.

dialysis A process used to clean blood; blood is filtered by passing it over a partially permeable membrane, dissolved substances diffuse from the blood through the membrane into a fluid on the other side and are removed.

diastolic pressure The pressure of the blood when the ventricles of the heart relax; it is generally lower than systolic pressure.

differentiation A process in which new cells develop specialised features to carry out a job.

diffusion The movement of a substance from a region of higher concentration to a region of lower concentration.

digestion The breakdown of food into smaller soluble molecules.

diploid Cells of organisms which contain chromosomes in pairs.

DNA The molecule that carries the genetic information in animals and higher plants; DNA is short for deoxyribonucleic acid.

DNA replication Copying of a DNA molecule to produce another, identical molecule.

double circulatory system A circulatory system where the blood passes through the heart twice – once to supply the body and once to supply the lungs.

double helix Two helices wound around each other, e.g. the structure of a DNA molecule.

E

ecological niche The place or function of a given organism within its ecosystem.

ecosystem The collection of different organisms in an area together with the important non-living factors such as water supply and temperature.

embryo transplantation To move an embryo from one mother, or laboratory vessel, to the uterus of a surrogate mother.

endangered A species close to extinction.

enzyme Special protein found in living organisms that speeds up the rate of a chemical reaction.

epidermis The outer layer of the skin.

epithelium The layer of cells lining a surface, e.g. the surface of a leaf or the lining of the nasal cavities.

eutrophication Rapid growth of algae due to an increase in nutrients in the water.

evaporation When a liquid changes to a gas, it evaporates.

evolution The gradual change in living organisms over millions of years caused by random mutations and natural selection.

excretion Getting rid of wastes made by the body.

exponential growth Extremely rapid growth that gets faster as time goes on.

extinct When all members of a species have died out.

F

fermentation Breakdown of food by microorganisms that does not require oxygen.

fertilisation When male and female gametes join together, e.g. pollen and ovules in flowers or sperm and eggs in mammals.

fertiliser A substance added to the ground by gardeners and farmers to help plants grow.

flaccid Plant cell that has lost water and is no longer turgid.

food chain A simple diagram using arrows to show the feeding relationships between some plants and animals.

food web A diagram showing how all of the food chains in an area link together.

fossil Preserved evidence of a dead animal or plant; fossils can be body parts or evidence of activity such as tracks, burrows, nests or teeth marks.

G

gamete Special cells that join to form a new individual during sexual reproduction .

gaseous exchange The movement of gases across an exchange membrane, e.g. in the lungs of mammals, usually involving carbon dioxide and oxygen moving in opposite directions.

gene A length of DNA that tells growing cells how to make particular chemicals; genes help to determine the eventual structure and behaviour of an organism.

gene pool The total number of genes available to a species in a local population.

genetic code The sequence of bases in DNA that carries the information needed to create an organism.

genetic engineering A range of technologies that allow scientists to transfer genes from one living organism to another.

genetic modification (GM) The addition of genes from one organism to another species using DNA technology.

genetically identical Having exactly the same genes, i.e. being clones.

geotropism Growing towards the centre of the Earth.

germination The first stages of growth of a seed into a new plant.

gestation The time between conception and birth, e.g. in humans this is pregnancy, which lasts for roughly 42 weeks.

guard cells Cells which change shape to open or close the stomata in leaves.

H

habitat A place where an animal or plant lives.

haemoglobin A complex chemical found in red blood cells that transports oxygen around the body by combining with it.

hallucinogen A drug such as LSD that gives the user hallucinations.

haploid number The number of chromosomes present in the sperm or egg of a species.

herbivore An animal that eats plants.

heterozygous An individual with two different alleles for an inherited feature.

homeostasis Keeping a constant internal environment.

homologous A matched pair of chromosomes; humans have 22 homologous pairs of chromosomes and a pair of sex chromosomes.

homozygous An individual with two alleles that are the same for an inherited feature, e.g. a blue-eyed person will have two alleles coding for blue eye colour.

hormone A chemical produced by an endocrine gland which changes the way other parts of the body work; hormones pass around the body in the blood.

host An organism that is carrying another one inside its body.

humus Decayed remains of animal and plant material in the soil.

hybrid An organism made when two different species breed together.

hydroponics Growing plants in mineral solutions without the need for soil.

hypothermia A condition caused by the body getting too cold. Hypothermia can lead to death if untreated.

I

immobilised enzyme Enzyme covered in a chemical such as alginate.

immune system The parts of the body that protect against illnesses; the lymph glands are particularly important in the immune system.

indicator species A species that is particularly sensitive to an environmental pollution; the presence or absence of indicator species is often used to assess the degree of pollution in an environment.

infertility Unable to produce offspring.

inherit To receive something from your parents, usually used to describe characteristics that can be passed down through sperm and eggs.

intensive farming Farming that uses a lot of artificial fertilisers and energy to produce a high yield per farm worker.

invertebrate An animal without a backbone.

K

kwashiorkor An illness caused by protein deficiency due to lack of food; sufferers often have swollen bellies caused by retention of fluid in the abdomen.

L

lactic acid A toxic chemical produced by anaerobic respiration in animals.

lactose intolerance Being allergic to lactose, a sugar found in milk and many dairy products.

legume A plant with root nodules that can fix nitrogen from the air, e.g. bean and pea plants.

lignin A complex, waterproof substance laid down in the walls of xylem vessels.

limiting factor A factor that prevents a reaction from speeding up. At low light levels the light keeps the rate of photosynthesis low - an increase in the light intensity will produce a rise in the rate of photosynthesis. At higher light levels another factor, e.g. carbon dioxide levels, may be limiting. At this stage a rise in light levels will have no effect on the rate of photosynthesis.

ligaments Tissue that joins two bones together.

lipase An enzyme that can digest fat.

lysis To split apart.

M

malignant A malignant tumour is one whose cells can spread into other tissues and cause more tumours.

meiosis A specialised form of cell division that produces cells called gametes carrying half the usual number of chromosomes which are used in sexual reproduction.

menstruation The release of blood and cells from the body of a female when the wall of the uterus breaks down.

microorganism An organism that is only visible under a microscope.

mineral deficiency Lack of essential minerals in the diet of animals or in the soil of plants.

mitochondria Cell structures that carry out aerobic respiration releasing energy.

mitosis The process of cell division that forms new genetically identical cells.

monocular Having only one eye or eyepiece; many microscopes and telescopes are monocular.

mutation A random change in the genotype of an organism; mutations are almost always disadvantageous.

mutualism Two different species live together but both benefit, e.g. cleaner species.

N

natural selection Factors in the environment affect animals and plants so that some survive to reproduce successfully and pass on their good combinations of genes. Others survive less well and do not pass on their poor combinations of genes as often.

negative feedback When the output from a process tends to slow down the speed of the process.

neurone A nerve cell.

nitrifying bacteria Bacteria that convert ammonia to nitrites and nitrates.

nitrogen-fixing bacteria Bacteria that take in nitrogen gas and produce complex nitrogen-containing chemicals.

nuclear transfer Moving the nucleus from one cell into another cell that has had its nucleus removed.

O

oestrogen A female hormone produced by the ovary.

optimum pH The pH range that produces the best reaction rate.

optimum temperature The temperature range that produces the best reaction rate.

organic farmer A farmer who avoids artificial fertilisers, pesticides and energy inputs and uses natural cycles and materials to increase yield.

osmosis Net movement of water across a partially permeable membrane from an area of high water concentration to an area of low water concentration.

ossification The formation of bone from cartilage.

osteoporosis A condition in older people, particularly women, where calcium-containing minerals leave the bone, making it thinner, more brittle and so more likely to break.

P

pacemaker Group of cells in the heart that stimulates the heart muscle to contract.

parasite An organism that gets its food from another organism, called the host, without killing it.

partially permeable A membrane that allows some small molecules to pass through but not larger molecules.

passive immunity When antibodies are given in a vaccine and the body is able to defend itself against a pathogen for a short time.

pathogen An organism that causes a disease.

performance enhancer Drug used to improve performance in a sporting event.

pesticide A chemical designed to kill a pest; different types of pesticides kill rats, rabbits, worms or insects.

phloem Specialised transporting cells in a plant which form tubules to carry sugars from the leaves to other parts.

photosynthesis The production, in green plants, of sugar and oxygen from carbon dioxide and water using light energy.

phototropism Growth of plants towards a source of light.

placebo A treatment with no active ingredient used in drug trials.

placenta The organ which allows materials to be exchanged between a mother and a foetus in the uterus.

plankton Microscopic organisms that live in water: zooplankton are animals and phytoplankton are plants.

plasma The liquid part of the blood.

plasmolysis The shrinking of a plant cell due to loss of water, the cell membrane pulls away from the cell wall.

platelet Found in the blood and involved in clotting.

pollination The transfer of pollen (male gametes) from one flower to another.

population Group of animals or plants of the same species.

predator Animal that hunts and kills other animals for food.

preserve To prevent something decaying.

prey Animals that are hunted by other animals.

producer An organism that makes organic material; green plants are primary producers because they use energy in sunlight to make sugar.

progesterone Female hormone produced by the ovary.

protease An enzyme that can digest protein.

pyramid of biomass A diagram to show the masses of living organisms present at each trophic level in an ecosystem.

pyramid of numbers A diagram to show the number of living organisms present at each trophic level in an ecosystem.

Q

quadrat Frames or pointers used to mark out a sample of an area for more intensive study.

R

RDA Recommended daily allowance of a foodstuff that dieticians recommend for a healthy diet, e.g. of a vitamin.

recessive A feature which does not appear when a gene contains two different alleles for the feature.

residual capacity Amount of air that cannot be breathed out of the lungs.

respiration The chemical process that releases energy from food in the cells of a living organisms.

S

saprophyte An organism that breaks down dead organic matter, usually used to refer to fungi.

selective breeding Two organisms with desirable characteristics mated together to produce offspring with a combination of the desired characteristics.

species A group of living things that can interbreed and produce fertile offspring.

specificity Needing a particular thing, e.g. enzymes show specificity as they only react with a particular, or specific, substrate.

stem cell A cell found in embryos that can develop into any other type of cell.

stomata Small holes in the surface of leaves which allow gases in and out of leaves.

sustainable development Development that does not make it more difficult for the generations that come after us.

sustainable resource Resource that will not run out because it is being produced at the same rate as it is being used.

synapse The gap between two nerve cells.

systolic pressure The pressure of the blood when the ventricles of the heart contract; it is generally higher than diastolic pressure.

T

tendon Tissue that joins a muscle to a bone.

testosterone Male hormone made by the testes.

tidal air Amount of air taken in and breathed out when a person is at rest.

toxin A poison, usually used to mean a poison produced by a living organism.

transgenic organism Organism that contains DNA from another organism.

transpiration The release of water vapour from a plant through the leaves.

transplant To put an organ from one organism into another.

trophic The level at which an organism gets its food; primary producers are level one, primary consumers are level two and secondary consumers are level three.

turgid Plant cells that are full of water with their walls bowed out and pushing against neighbouring cells.

turgor pressure The pressure exerted on the cell membrane by the cell wall when the cell is fully inflated.

U

urea A substance made by the liver to remove excess proteins.

urine Liquid waste made by the kidney.

V

vacuole A sac in a cell filled with a watery solution; plant cells tend to have large vacuoles but animal cells have small ones.

valve Stops back-flow of blood in the heart.

variation The existence of a range of individuals of the same group with different characteristics.

vascular bundle A collection of xylem and phloem vessels in a plant, they can be seen in leaves as the veins.

vasoconstriction Narrowing of the small blood vessels in the skin, making the skin look white and reducing heat loss from the body.

vasodilation Widening of the small blood vessels in the skin, making the skin look pink or flushed and increasing heat loss from the body.

vein A blood vessel carrying blood towards the heart.

ventricle Large muscular chamber in the heart.

vertebrate An animal with a backbone or spine.

villus A small projection on the inner surface of the gut to increase the surface area and so speed up absorption.

vital capacity Total amount of air that can be breathed out after taking in the maximum amount of air.

X

XX chromosomes The sex chromosomes present in a human female.

XY chromosomes The sex chromosomes present in a human male.

xylem Cells specialised for transporting water through a plant; xylem cells are dead, have thick walls, no cytoplasm and their end walls have broken down so they form a continuous tube.

Z

zygote A cell produced when a male and female gamete join.

Answers

Here are the answers to the topic questions from the revision guide pages, and the answers to the exam-practice questions in the workbook.

This section is perforated, so that you can remove the answers to help test yourself or a friend.

B1 Understanding ourselves

Page 4
1. glucose → lactic acid + energy.
2. They need to repay the oxygen debt.
3. Breathing and heart rate.
4. Age, diet and amount of exercise.

Page 5
1. $80 \times 0.75 - 60$ g
2. They contain images of thin people that influence a person's view of themselves.
3. They break down large food molecules into small soluble molecules.
4. Emulsification increases the surface area. Digestion breaks down the molecules.

Page 6
1. They carry pathogens from one host to another.
2. Malignant tumours are cancer cells, which divide out of control and spread around the body. Benign cells are slow to divide and harmless.
3. They lock onto antigens causing the bacteria to stick together.
4. In a blind trial, volunteers do not know which treatment they are receiving. In a double blind trial, the doctors also do not know which treatment is used.

Page 7
1. The iris.
2. The ciliary muscles become less flexible.
3. Stimulus, receptor, sensory neurone, CNS, motor neurone, effector, response.
4. Transmitter is only made on one side of the synapse.

Page 8
1. LSD.
2. It stimulates the acetylcholine receptors, allowing more impulses to pass.
3. Cigarette smoke stops the cilia from moving. Dust and particulates collect and irritate the cells. Smokers cough to move this mess upwards so it can be swallowed.
4. They block the exchange of gases and reduce the amount of oxygen available to the rest of the body.

Page 9
1. It is when body temperature falls too low.
2. It is widening of the blood vessels.
3. Hair growth in the pubic area or under the arms.

Page 10
1. Four.
2. 35.
3. T.
4. DNA codes for an enzyme, and the enzyme controls the reaction that makes the pigment to colour the eye.

Page 11
1. They are genetically identical.
2. One from: radiation, chemicals, they occur spontaneously.
3. Blue.
4.

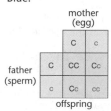

B2 Understanding our environment

Page 13
1. It suffocates.
2. a Herbicide b pesticide.
3. A group of animals or plants of the same species.
4. Use numbers as coordinates.

Page 14
1. To trap light or for photosynthesis or make food.
2. They have no chloroplasts or they can't make their own food.
3. So they can survive in water.
4. Felidae.

Page 15
1. Any three from: respiration (energy), storage, make proteins, make cellulose.
2.

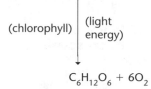

$$6CO_2 + 6H_2O \xrightarrow[\text{(chlorophyll)}]{\text{(light energy)}} C_6H_{12}O_6 + 6O_2$$

3. Keeping the plants warm, providing the plants with extra carbon dioxide, increasing the amount of light for the plant.
4. It is produced from respiration but not needed in photosynthesis.

Page 16
1. So the species survives.
2. There is increased competition from the grey squirrel.
3. A relationship where both organisms benefit.
4. There is more food, so the owls can raise more young.

Page 17
1. To stop sand getting in their eyes.
2. They are large to spread load on snow, and have fur on the sole for grip and insulation.
3. To reduce water loss.
4. To attract insects.

Page 18
1. One from: some body parts decay quickly before they can be fossilised; fossilisation is rare, most living things will completely decay; there may still be fossils we have not found.
2. Organisms were created, they did not evolve.
3. In their genes.
4. Within any species there is variation. There will be competition for limited resources such as food. Only those best adapted will survive, called survival of the fittest. Successful adaptations are passed to the next generation in genes. Over time, the changes may result in a new species. The less well adapted species may become extinct.

Page 19
1. Sulphur dioxide.
2. The USA uses more fossil fuels (oil, gas coal).
3. Any two from: bloodworm, water louse, sludge worm, rat-tailed maggot.
4. It cannot tolerate the low oxygen levels found in polluted water.

Page 20
1. They may be unable to adapt to the change fast enough.
2. For example, local food or dances could be preserved as entertainment for tourists.
3. The whales lose their freedom.
4. For example, prevent the import of wood from unsustainable forests or provide money for local communities to find alternative incomes to deforestation.

B3 Living and growing

Page 22
1. Amino acids are joined together.
2. Three.
3. An enzyme is a protein that acts as a biological catalyst.
4. It denatures the enzyme, changing the shape of the active site.

Page 23
1. The movement of molecules from a high to a low concentration.
2. They increase the surface area, which speeds up diffusion.
3. It carries a signal from one neurone to the next.
4. It diffuses through the stomata.

Page 24
1. Haemoglobin.
2. Pulmonary artery.
3. To withstand high pressure.
4. Blood going to the body can be pumped at a much higher pressure than blood going to the lungs.

Page 25
1. If the cell is too large it could not absorb enough food and oxygen through the surface of its membrane to stay alive.
2. 23 pairs or 46.
3. Meiosis.
4. Both make new cells, at one point single strands move to opposite poles.

Page 26
1. Any two from: cell wall, chloroplast, large vacuole.
2. They are easier to grow.
3. They are bigger so they need time to develop enough to survive outside the uterus.
4. Digestive system problems.

Page 27
1. It makes roots grow.
2. The root.
3. It causes elongation of the cells.
4. It causes elongation of the cells on the dark side.

Page 28
1. Choose the characteristic. Cross-breed. Select the best offspring. Repeat the selection and breeding process for a number of generations.
2. There is a reduction in variation; more chance of harmful recessive genes being expressed.
3. There may be harmful effects on humans who eat them.

4 Select the characteristic. Identify and isolate the gene. Insert the gene into chromosome of a different organism. Replicate (copy) the gene in the organism and produce the protein.

Page 29

1 Embryo transplantation.
2 Nuclear transfer.
3 One from: the plants are all genetically identical, if the environment changes or a new disease breaks out it is unlikely that any of the plants will survive; cloning plants over many years has resulted in little genetic variation.
4 Plants with the desired characteristics are chosen. A large number of small pieces of tissue are taken from the parent plant. They are put into sterile test tubes that contain growth medium. The tissue pieces are left in suitable conditions to grow into plants.

B4 It's a green world

Page 31

1 Palisade cells.
2 They allow gases to diffuse easily and reach all the cells.
3 So it has a large surface area to absorb light.
4 To allow gas exchange.

Page 32

1 Osmosis.
2 Water leaves the cells, which become plasmolysed.
3 Less sugar is made, water leaves the guard cell, the guard cell becomes plasmolysed, the stoma closes.
4 To reduce water loss.

Page 33

1 Xylem vessels.
2 They contain lignin.
3 Any two from: increased light intensity, increased temperature, increased air movement (wind), a fall in humidity (amount of water in the atmosphere).
4 When light intensity increases the stomata open. This allows more water to escape.

Page 34

1 Potassium and magnesium.
2 Phosphorus.
3 Magnesium.
4 Active transport requires energy and is against the concentration gradient; it also uses carrier molecules.

Page 35

1 A pyramid of numbers shows the number of organisms, a pyramid of biomass shows the mass of the organisms.
2 $\frac{40}{2000} = 0.02$ or 2%.
3 Sugar cane is fermented using yeast to make alcohol. The alcohol is mixed with petrol to make Gasohol, a fuel for cars.

4 The plants used can be replaced by growing more.

Page 36

1 Suggestions such as: enclosed in very small spaces, given harmful drugs, etc.
2 The mineral supply is controlled and unused minerals are recycled, reducing costs. There is better control of external conditions and disease.
3 One from: grow nitrogen-fixing plants, use manure, use compost.
4 One from: high costs, small yield.

Page 37

1 Earthworms, maggots and woodlice.
2 The temperature at which enzymes work best.
3 An organism that feeds off dead and decaying material.
4 It removes the moisture that bacteria need for growth.

Page 38

1 Photosynthesis.
2 Limestone reacts with acid rain to release carbon dioxide.
3 A decomposer.
4 One from: nitrogen-fixing bacteria convert it into ammonia or nitrates; lightning combines nitrogen and oxygen to form oxides, the oxides dissolve in rain and form nitrates in the soil.

B5 The living body

Page 40

1 Cartilage.
2 Ossification.
3 As one muscle contracts the other relaxes, they pull the arm in opposite directions.
4 The elbow acts as a pivot and although the muscle contracts for only a short distance, the hand moves much further.

Page 41

1 Lungs.
2 Heart relaxes, blood enters the atrium, atria contract pushing blood into the ventricles, ventricles contract pushing blood out into the arteries.
3 To send electrical impulses to the heart and regulate the heartbeat.
4 To send impulses across the atria causing them to contract.

Page 42

1 The valves can be replaced by artificial valves or valves from a donor.
2 Lowers blood pressure.
3 So more organs are available for transplants, solve the shortage of suitable organs.

4 Antibodies in plasma of group O cause the donated red blood cells with antigen A to agglutinate (clump together).

Page 43

1 They contract.
2 Large surface area, rich blood supply.
3 It caused asbestosis.
4 More mucus is produced forming a plug.

Page 44

1 Liver.
2 Because glucose is reabsorbed against a concentration gradient.
3 Water in sweat uses the heat energy to evaporate.
4 Low concentration of blood sensed by receptors in the hypothalamus, pituitary gland stops producing ADH, less water reabsorbed by the kidney tubule.

Page 45

1 The lining is shed.
2 Controls the release of the egg.
3 So they can be tested for certain birth defects.
4 IVF does not have a very high success rate, multiple births are a problem.

Page 46

1 So the body does not react to them.
2 Advances and experience in new medical techniques.
3 Difficulty in finding tissues or blood that matches or that there is a shortage of donors.
4 Prevent the immune system rejecting transplant as foreign tissue.

Page 47

1 5.4 to 8.4 kg.
2 Makes the body release more growth hormones.
3 Modern treatments and cures for many diseases, fewer deaths from industrial diseases, healthier diet and lifestyle, better housing conditions.
4 Triggers an increased production of cartilage causing an increase in length of long bones in the arms and legs.

B6 Beyond the microscope

Page 49

1 To help them move.
2 Hydrogen sulphide or ammonia.
3 To kill any unwanted bacteria already in the milk.
4 Wash hands before and after handling bacteria, disinfect working areas, sterilise all equipment before and after use, never leave the lids off containers.

Page 50

1 Drinking contaminated water.
2 *Salmonella* and *E. coli*.
3 Penicillin.
4 Food cannot be kept cold, so decays faster.

Page 51

1 Sugar → alcohol + carbon dioxide + energy.
2 To stop the yeast carrying out aerobic respiration and not make any alcohol.
3 Distillation, heating the drink to evaporate the alcohol then cooling the alcohol to collect it.
4 By using different strains of yeast.

Page 52

1 Because it caries on without stopping for a long time, methane is taken out continuously not just in one go.
2 Above 45 °C enzymes denature and bacteria die.
3 Heats water and produces steam.
4 Biofuels do not increase atmospheric levels of carbon dioxide and growing the plants may help to reduce levels.

Page 53

1 It aerates the soil and improves drainage.
2 Earthworms mix up the layers; this results in a deeper layer of fertile soil.
3 Millipedes or springtails.
4 Convert nitrogen from the air and use it in their own proteins.

Page 54

1 Reduces the competition for food between young and adult.
2 When it swims in fresh water.
3 Not enough oxygen for them to survive.
4 Algae have more light energy for photosynthesis.

Page 55

1 Proteases.
2 Glucose and fructose.
3 Immobilised enzymes are easier to separate from the solution and they do not contaminate the product.
4 Glucose and galactose.

Page 56

1 Identify the gene needed and remove it from the DNA; cut open the DNA in another organism; add the gene to the DNA of that organism, this is now a transgenic organism; clone the transgenic organism.
2 Cut open the DNA.
3 Bacteria.
4 The resistance could pass to plants (weeds) in the environment making it more difficult to kill them.

Workbook answers

B1 Understanding ourselves

Page 62 Fit for life

1 a i Lactic acid
ii Body needs more energy; not enough oxygen in muscles; anaerobic respiration takes place
b Takes in extra oxygen to break down the lactic acid; repay oxygen debt
2 Bacteria/viruses can still enter body
3 a Take more exercise; eat a balanced diet; lose weight; drink less alcohol; relax more   *(Any 2 = 1 mark each)*
b Small blood vessels may burst in brain; causing a stroke; blood vessels in kidney may burst   *(Any 2 = 1 mark each)*

Page 63 What's for lunch?

1 a Kwashiorkor
b RDA = 40 x 0.75
= 30 g
2 a More exercise
b Meat is a good source of essential amino acids or vitamin B1; he will need to eat alternatives

3 a

food type	enzyme	product
protein	protease	amino acids
fat	lipase	fatty acids and glycerol

(1 mark for each correct box)

b Bile emulsifies the fat; breaking it up into smaller droplets; lipase enzyme then breaks up the fat molecules; into fatty acids and glycerol   *(Any 3)*

Page 64 Keeping healthy

1 a i Vector   **ii** Feeds off living host
b Drain stagnate water to kill larva; put oil on water to prevent larva from breathing; spray insecticide to kill adult; take Larium to kill protozoan   *(Any 1)*
2 a Active: given pathogen; body makes antibodies; long lasting; passive: given antibodies; body does not learn how to make antibodies; short lived
b Harmless pathogen contains antigen; body learns how to make correct antibody
c i Do not kill virus; only treat bacterial or fungal infections
ii Bacteria are becoming resistant
iii Some patients take the new drug; others take the placebo; without knowing

Page 65 Keeping in touch

1 a

part of the eye	function
retina	contains light receptors
optic nerve	carries impulses to brain
cornea	refracts light

b Allows it to judge distance
c Ciliary muscle relaxes; suspensory muscle pulls; lens thin
d Concave lens; glasses; contact lenses; cornea surgery
(Any 2)
2 a 3: sensory neurone; 4: relay neurone; 5: motor neurone
b Impulse triggers release transmitter substance; transmitter substance (acetylrcholine) diffuses across synapse; binds with receptors; triggers impulse in second neurone
(Any 2 = 1 mark each)

Page 66 Drugs and you

1 a

type of drug	example
hallucinogen	cannabis
depressant	alcohol

(2 correct = 2; 1 correct = 1 mark)

b For: used as a pain killer; may prevent drug crimes; against: may lead to use of more dangerous drugs
2 a Stops cilia moving; dust collects; leads to smokers' cough
b Stimulates the receptors; allows more impulses to pass
3 a Matthew; because he drinks 5 units and Jo drinks only 4 units
b More people drink at weekend; excessive drinking leads to more accidents

Page 67 Staying in balance

1 a Get too hot; start to sweat; lose too much water
b Hypothermia
c Blood capillaries in skin dilate; increasing blood flow
d Body gets too hot mechanisms (e.g. sweating) cool body; body cools switching off mechanisms (stop sweating)
2 a Diabetes
b Diet/insulin injections
3 a Increases thickness
b Maintains levels
c Given sex hormones

Page 68 Gene control

1 a Nucleus; genes; DNA
2 a 10
b 20
c Have 23 chromosomes not 10
d Gene is switched off in nucleus of ear cells
3 a 4
b 30; because A always links to a T
c Base sequence would be different; different amino acid coded for; amino acids will form different protein (enzyme); incorrect enzyme so pigment cannot be made
(Any 3 = 1 mark each)

Page 69 Who am I?

1 a

egg	sperm	fertilised egg	gender of child
X	X	XX	girl
X	Y	XY	boy

(1 mark each)

b Only males have Y chromosome; only sperm can carry X or Y; eggs can only carry X chromosome
(Any 2 = 1 mark each)
2 a Radiation; chemicals (e.g. tobacco smoke)   *(Any 1)*
b Base sequence would be different; different amino acid coded for; amino acids will form different protein; incorrect protein so blood cannot clot
(Any 2 = 1 mark each)
3 a Purple because F$_1$ are all purple
b i

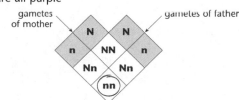

ii *(Ring round nn)*

B2 Understanding our environment

Page 71 Ecology in our school grounds
1 a i Too cold; no food *(Any 1)*
  ii Difficult to reach so difficult to explore
 b i The range of living things in an ecosystem
  ii Using pesticides kills the invertebrates; less food for the vertebrates; so their number also falls
    (Any 2 = 1 mark each)

2 a $\dfrac{20 \times 10}{5} = 40$

 b i Set more traps; over larger area
  ii Larger sample size; be more representative of the whole wood not just a small area

Page 72 Grouping organisms
1 a i Birds   **ii** Beak; feathers
 b No backbone
 c

	food	shape	movement
animals	eat food	compact	move around

2 a Hybrid   **b** It is not a species
3 a Organisms that interbreed; produce fertile offspring
 b i Bobcat; ocelot
  ii First part of Latin name the same

Page 73 The food factory
1 a $6CO_2 + 6H_2O \rightarrow C_6H_{12}O_6 + 6O_2$
 b

product of photosynthesis	use in the plant
cellulose	cell wall
protein	growth/repair
oil	storage

2 a Carbon dioxide; temperature
 b i As light intensity increases the rate increases; until point B when it levels off
3 a Respiration
 b Need the energy it provides to live

Page 74 Compete or die
1 a The place an organism occupies within its ecosystem
 b i Grey squirrels out-compete red
  ii Increase in numbers
2 a i Decrease
  ii More caterpillars; so more get eaten
 b i Organism that feeds off another living organism
  ii Mutualism
3 Population starts to rise because plenty of food; population starts to fall; because of increase in predator number; predator number falls so lemming population can rise again
  (Any 3 = 1 mark each)

Page 75 Adapt to fit
1 a

adaptation	why it helps the camel survive
no fat on body, except in hump	whole body not insulated
hair-lined nostrils	stop sand getting into nose
higher body temperatures do not harm camel	higher body temperature reduces need to sweat

 b i Layer of fat; for insulation; small ears; reduce heat loss; fur on soles; insulate feet
    (Any 3 = 1 mark each)
  ii Adapted to different habitats; cannot compete with brown bear in warmer habitat
2 a Reduces surface area; so reduced water loss
 b Colourful petals; nectar; sticky pollen *(Any 1)*
 c Pollen is smaller; feathery stigma; no nectar; no colour to flowers *(Any 2 = 1 mark each)*

Page 76 Survival of the fittest
1 a (B) C D A
  (C before D = 1; D before A = 1; A at end = 1 mark)
 b Some body parts decay and do not survive; some fossils have not been discovered yet; fossilisation is rare
  (Any 2 = 1 mark each)
 c For: complex organisms appear then disappear/there are gaps in fossil record; against: there are examples of gradual change seen in the fossil record e.g. horse
2 a Organisms better adapted are more likely to survive
 b More resistant bacteria survive; pass on resistance

Page 77 Population out of control?
1 a Climate change/greenhouse effect; melting ice caps; rise in sea level *(Any 2 = 1 mark each)*
 b i CFC
  ii More ultra violet rays get through
2 a Exponential growth
 b Developed countries use more fuel per person; developed countries have more cars; developed countries have more factories; developed countries have more fossil-fuelled power stations *(Any 2 = 1 mark each)*
3 a Indicator species
 b Mussels, damselfly larva and bloodworms survive in polluted water; if it was clean you would find alderfly and stonefly

Page 78 Sustainability
1 Loss of habitat; hunted; other animals out-competed it; disease; habitat polluted *(Any 2 = 1 mark each)*
2 a Captive breeding programs/prevent hunting to extinction
 b Tourism; improved transport; improved water supply/other resources *(Any 2 = 1 mark each)*
3 a For: provide food/jobs; against: whales could become extinct
 b Area too large to police
4 a Leaves enough fish behind to breed; maintain population
 b Alternative to fossil fuels; can easily be replaced; because they grow fast *(Any 2 = 1 mark each)*

B3 Living and growing

Page 80 Molecules of life

1 Mitochondria

2 a James; pattern is identical

b DNA isolated; DNA cut into fragment; fragments separated; by electric current/ electrophoresis; banding compared with a reference *(Any 3 = 1 mark each)*

c i 5

ii ATATACATTTTTGTT

3 a Biological catalyst; that speeds up reactions in body

b As temperature increases the rate increases; until 40 °C when it falls

c 40–42 °C/any temperature in this range

d High temperature denatures enzyme; enzyme changes shape; so can no longer fit substrate

Page 81 Diffusion

1 a Movement of substances; from a region of high concentration to low concentration

b Increasing surface area; decreasing diffusion distance; greater concentration difference

2 a Carbon dioxide; waste

b Alveoli

3 Higher concentration of carbon dioxide in the air; diffuses through stomata; used in photosynthesis; which keeps concentration low in leaf *(Any 3 = 1 mark each)*

4 Releases transmitter substance; transmitter substance diffuses across gap; transmitter triggers impulse in next neurone

Page 82 Keep it moving

1 a Disc-shaped: large surface area takes up oxygen quicker; no nucleus: more space to carry more oxygen

b Haemoglobin

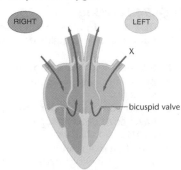

2 a i *(See diagram)*

ii *(See diagram)*

b Needs to pump blood further; at higher pressure

c i Rejection; waiting for donor; need for anti-rejection drugs *(Any 2 = 1 mark each)*

ii Advantage: no need to replace batteries; disadvantage: have to wait for suitable donor

3 a Arteries transport blood away from heart; capillaries allow the exchange of materials with tissue; veins transport blood back to heart

b Blood going to body can be pumped at much higher pressure; provides greater flow to all organs

Page 83 Divide and rule

1 a Limits size organism can grow to; no cell differentiation; unable to form complex tissue e.g. nerves

(Any 2 = 1 mark each)

b i

cube	surface area in cm^2	volume in cm^3	ratio
A	24	8	24/8 = 3
B	54	27	54/27 = 2
C	96	64	96/64 = 1.5
D	150	125	150/125 = 1.2

ii Larger cells have much smaller surface are compared to volume; difficult to absorb enough food/oxygen

2 a Mitosis

b Cells are diploid; chromosomes separate to opposite poles

3 a Contains enzymes; to break down egg membrane

b i Meiosis

ii Homologous chromosomes separate; haploid cells form; variation occurs/new cells are different from each other; four cells produced *(Any 1 = 1 mark)*

c Only contain one of each pair of chromosomes/ contain half the number of chromosomes found in body cells

Page 84 Growing up

1 a Similar: both have cytoplasm/cell membrane; different: plant cell has cell wall/vacuole/chloroplasts

b i Stem cells

ii Embryos die; unethical; religious beliefs

(Any 2 = 1 mark each)

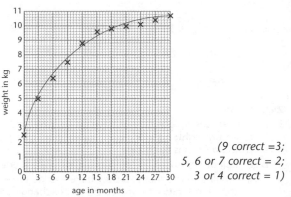

(9 correct =3;
5, 6 or 7 correct = 2;
3 or 4 correct = 1)

2 a i *(See diagram)*

ii *(See diagram)*

iii Weight increases; as age increases

iv Infancy

b Poor diet/problems with digestive system

Page 85 Controlling plant growth

1 a Stimulates root growth

b i Speeds up growth too much; so they die

ii Narrow leaves; they do not absorb as much weedkiller

2 a i Geotropism

ii Because it grows in the same direction as gravity

b i Auxin

ii Produced in tip; more collects on the dark side; causes cell elongation on dark side

iii No tip; so no auxin produced

Page 86 New genes for old

1 a Select characteristics; cross-breed; select the best offspring; breed these offspring over many generations *(Any 3 = 1 mark each)*

2 a TG just before AAA have swapped round to GT

b Change in base sequence that codes for enzyme B; protein (enzyme) made is the wrong shape; red pigment cannot be turned into purple

3 a Find the gene for beta-carotene in carrots; remove gene; put gene into rice

b Advantage: produces organisms with new characteristics; disadvantage: may have harmful effects

Page 87 More of the same

1 a Sperm collected from bull; cows artificially inseminated; embryo collected; embryo cloned; embryo implanted in surrogate cow *(Any 3 = 1 mark each)*

b i Pig organs used for transplants instead of humans; reduces need to wait for donors to die

ii Breeding pigs just to kill them; may not want an animal's organ; religious reasons *(Any 1 = 1 mark)*

c i Nucleus removed from body cell; no fertilisation takes place; clone of the adult *(Any 2 = 1 mark each)*

ii B; because the nucleus came from cell from sheep B

2 a Advantage: characteristics all the same/mass produce plants quickly; disadvantage: susceptible to new disease/changes in the environment/lack variation

b Plant cell retains ability to differentiate; into all the different types of cells; easier to separate plant cells

B4 It's a green world
Page 89 Who planted that there?
1 a i–iii (See diagram)
  b (See diagram)

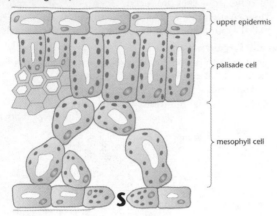

upper epidermis

palisade cell

mesophyll cell

2 Diffusion
3 a Thin so gases/light do not have far to travel; chlorophyll to absorb light; network veins for support/transport; stomata for gas exchange   (Any 3 = 1 mark each)
  b i Full of chloroplasts; to absorb a lot of light energy
    ii Small and irregular; so they have a large surface area to volume ratio; for increased gas exchange
    (Any 2 = 1 mark each)

Page 90 Water, water everywhere
1 a Higher concentration water inside potato; water moved out by osmosis
  b Take on water; and burst (lysis)
  c i Higher concentration of water outside cell; water moves into cell; increase in water pressure against cell wall; turgor pressure causes cell to be turgid
    (Any 2 = 1 mark each)
    ii Cell drawn with cytoplasm shrinking away from wall

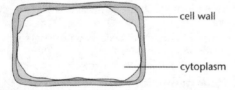

cell wall

cytoplasm

    iii Plasmolysed
2 a Photosynthesis; cooling; support   (Any 2 = 1 mark each)
  b Photosynthesis stops in dark; less sugar produced; water concentration in guard cell increases; water moves out by osmosis   (Any 3 = 1 mark each)

Page 91 Transport in plants
1 a A: phloem; B: xylem
  b Transport water/minerals; from root to leaves; support plant   (Any 2 = 1 mark each)
  c Contains lignin; for strength/cells die to make tubes; to carry water through   (Any 2 = 1 mark each)
2 a Any value below 7.4 g
  b i Lowers rate
    ii Increases humidity; which reduces evaporation

Page 92 Plants need minerals too
1 a

mineral	why the mineral is needed	how the mineral is used
phosphate	respiration or growth	used to make cell membranes or DNA
potassium	respiration or photosynthesis	make enzymes
magnesium	photosynthesis	make chlorophyll

  b i Phosphate: poor root growth; discoloured leaves
    ii Potassium: poor flower or fruit growth; discoloured leaves
    iii Magnesium: yellow leaves
2 a i 0.0825
    ii 0.01/0.0125
  b Because there is a greater concentration in the cells; compared to the pond water
  c Active transport
  d Provide energy; needed for active transport

Page 93 Energy flow
1 a Numbers of organisms at each stage of food chain
  b

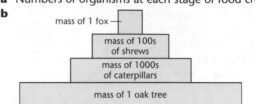

mass of 1 fox

mass of 100s of shrews

mass of 1000s of caterpillars

mass of 1 oak tree

  c Heat from respiration/egestion of waste/movement
2 a Use seeds for next year; use as biofuel
  b i 3090 – 1909 – 1022 = 159 kJ
    ii $\frac{159}{3090} \times 100 = 5.1\%$
  c More energy efficient
3 a Yeast is used to ferment the sugar; to produce alcohol; alcohol is mixed with petrol
  b Advantage: renewable energy source/cause less pollution/help countries become self reliant; disadvantage: can produce sulphur dioxide

Page 94 Farming
1 a DDT gets into plankton; passed along food chain; does not break down; builds up to toxic levels in seals
    (Any 3 = 1 mark each)
  b Less heat loss; less energy loss from movement
2 a By hydroponics; roots grow in water containing correct nutrients
  b Advantage: control mineral supply/conditions/disease so lower cost; disadvantage: manufactured fertiliser cost/tall plants need support
3 a Use of animal manure/compost; nitrogen fixing crops; seeding; growing seeds at different times
    (Any 2 = 1 mark each)
  b Cannot grow enough crops
  c i Biological control
    ii No predators so population keeps increasing

Page 95 Decay
1 a i 6.2 – 5.8 = 0.4
    ii Microorganisms had been killed
  b Breaks up remains; increasing surface area
  c i Bag C 40 °C
    ii Optimum temperature; for enzymes involved
  d Release enzymes onto food; enzymes digest food; fungi absorb digested food   (Any 2 = 1 mark each)
2 Kills bacteria/fungi by removing water

Page 96 Recycling
1 a i burning   ii respiration   iii photosynthesis
  b Photosynthesis
  c Carry out respiration; when they break down the dead plant and animal material
  d Turn into limestone; limestone weathered by acid rain; chemical reaction produces carbon dioxide
2 a To make proteins for growth
  b Break down dead plants and animals; turning nitrogen compounds into nitrates
  c Unreactive
  d Nitrogen-fixing bacteria; lightning
  e Denitrifying

B5 The living body

Page 98 In good shape

1 **a** Forms a framework; grows with the body; muscles can easily be attached; made from living tissue
(Any 2 = 1 mark each)
 b The shaft contains bone marrow.
 c Cartilage becomes bone; calcium and phosphate salts added
2 **a** Bones are soft/because of osteoporosis
 b Antagonistic
 c i Synovial
  ii Absorbs shock; acts as a lubricant
 d Advantage = more active/less pain;
 Disadvantage = danger of rejection/infection

Page 99 The vital pump

1 **a i** Aorta
  ii Pulmonary artery
 b Atria contract/blood pushed into ventricles; contraction is systole; ventricles contract/blood pushed out of heart; diastole occurs/heart relaxes to take in more blood
(Any 3 = 1 mark each)
2 **a i** Pacemaker/SAN/AVN
  ii SAN sends an impulse across atria; causes atria to contract; AVN sends impulse across ventricles; causes ventricles to contract *(Any 3 = 1 mark each)*
 b i ECG/electrocardiogram
  ii Echocardiogram
 c R

Page 100 Running repairs

1 **a** Oxygen; blocked; muscle; pressure
 b Smoking; reduces the amount of oxygen in blood/heart disease
 Stress; high blood pressure/kidney damage/stroke
 Alcohol; lower blood pressure/raise fat levels/cause blood clots
 Drugs; infection; heart attacks
(Any 3 = 1 mark each; must have at least one example linked to correct description; Max 2 marks from list of examples)
 c Haemoglobin
 d Changes shape to wrap round bacteria
2 Haemophilia is an inherited condition; Making cranberries part of your diet will help with blood clotting
3 **a** Group O
 b They have both A and B antigens; all other groups will have either A or B antibody; antibodies in the recipients blood react with AB antigens *(Any 2 = 1 mark each)*

Page 101 Breath of life

1 **a i** Amount of air that cannot be breathed out
  ii 3.5 (dm^3)
  iii 4 ÷ 12; × 60; 20 breaths per minute
(3 marks for correct answer)
 b Moist surface; thin lining; good blood supply/large number of capillaries *(Any 2 = 1 mark each)*
2 **a** Symptom = short of breath/wheezing/constriction of bronchioles; Treatment = inhaler/Ventolin
 b i 1–4
  ii Hayfever
3 **a** Cilia
 b Make mucus; (mucus) trap dust; cilia/hair-like structures move dust to throat *(Any 2 = 1 mark each)*

Page 102 Waste disposal

1 **a i** Renal artery
  ii Ureter
 b i A
  ii C
 c Made in the liver; from amino acids/proteins
 d i Anti-diuretic hormone/ADH
  ii When conditions return to normal; mechanism is switched off
2 Sweat evaporates
3 Forms carbonic acid; changes the pH of the blood; enzymes are affected by pH change/enzymes can't work efficiently
(Any 2 = 1 mark each)

Page 103 Life goes on

1 **a** Menstruation starts on day one/menstruation is the shedding of the uterus wall; ovulation happens between day 13 and 15/ovulation is release of egg; uterus lining gets thicker day 5–28/gets thinner 1–4
(Any 3 = 1 mark each)
 b FSH – starts egg development; LH – controls egg release; progesterone – controls thickness of uterus lining
2 **a** Egg is fertilised in lab/artificially; (fertilised) egg placed in uterus
 b Advantage = gives infertile couples chance of a baby; Disadvantage = low success rate/chance of multiple births/chance of surrogate mothers becoming attached to babies/baby may not carry genes of both parents
 c i Amniocentesis
  ii Thin needle; guided by ultrasound; through abdomen/into amniotic fluid *(Any 2 = 1 mark each)*
 d Cost of bringing up a child with special needs; life expectancy of child; if they can cope with taking care of the child *(Any 2 = 1 mark each)*

Page 104 New for old

1 **a** (Kidney) dialysis
 b Power supply; what materials to use; if the body reacts
(Any 2 = 1 mark each)
 c Introduction of immuno-suppressive drugs; greater experience of techniques; better medical equipment
(Any 2 = 1 mark each)
2 **a** Shortage of donors; tissue not matching; size or age of donor/recipient *(Any 2 = 1 mark each)*
 b Immuno-suppressive drugs; matching tissue type as close as possible
 c For = more organs will be available/cut down waiting lists/stops relatives having to make a decision at death of a loved one; Against = many people do not want their organs used/may have religious objections

Page 105 Size matters

1 **a i** 98 (cm)
  ii 103 – 98; 5 (cm)
2 **a i** Increasing
  ii Better treatment of illness; fewer industrial diseases/accidents; healthier diet; better housing/sanitation *(Any 2 = 1 mark each)*
 b Personal = deterioration of health/becoming burden to family; National = cost to health service/payment of pensions
3 **a** Pituitary
 b Stimulates it to produce another hormone/IGF-1

B6 Beyond the microscope

Page 107 Understanding bacteria

1 a Curved rod; spiral; rod   *(Any 2 = 1 mark each)*
  b i Binary fission
    ii Causes disease/makes us ill
  c Nitrogen
2 a i (B) A D C   *(A before D = 1 mark; D before C = 1 mark)*
    ii So that no unwanted bacteria grow in the yoghurt
  b i Stop infection
    ii To prevent contamination by bacteria in air/stop bacteria escaping

Page 108 Harmful microorganisms

1 a Pathogen
  b Incubation period
  c i 2003
    ii More countries reporting cases, the more cases there were
    iii Number of cases went up but the number of countries went down
2 a i Alexander Fleming
    ii Fungus
  b Sprayed wounds; with carbolic acid; this was the first antiseptic   *(Any 2 = 1 mark each)*
  c i Dysentery; cholera
    ii Food cannot be stored/food decays faster/hospitals cannot function efficiently

Page 109 Microorganisms – factories for the future?

1 a Right amount of food; optimum pH; removal of waste products   *(Any 2 = 1 mark each)*
  b Yeast breaks down the sugar
  c So it carries out anaerobic respiration; (anaerobic respiration) is needed for alcohol production; stop it carrying out aerobic respiration; (aerobic respiration) makes water (not alcohol)   *(Any 2 = 1 mark each)*
2 a i Make the liquid clear/make the yeast settle out
    ii Kill any harmful bacteria
  b Heat to evaporate alcohol; cool to turn alcohol back into a liquid
  c i A; because growth is still increasing at the end
    ii Different strains result in different flavours
    iii Developed method of pasteurisation; so wine can be kept longer

Page 110 Biofuels

1 a Continuous flow
  b i Higher the temperature higher the volume of gas produced; until 45 °C; when amount of gas starts to fall with increased temperature   *(Any 2 = 1 mark each)*
    ii As temperature increases, enzymes work faster/better; above 45 °C; enzymes denature
  c Box A = fatty acids and amino acids; Box B = methane and carbon dioxide
2 a Recycles carbon dioxide instead of increasing levels in air; no particulates produced
  b Destroys habitats; animals may become extinct; burning increases carbon dioxide levels   *(Any 2 = 1 mark each)*

Page 111 Life in soil

1 a It aerates soil; improves drainage; mixes the layers; buries organic material so bacteria/fungi can decay it   *(Any 3 = 1 mark each)*
  b Earthworms mix up the layers; sub-soil mixes with decaying material; fertile layer becomes deeper   *(Any 2 = 1 mark each)*
  c Separates soil particles; creating air spaces; improves drainage; more oxygen available (for roots)   *(Any 3 = 1 mark each)*

2 a So it is available for plants to use
  b i Slug/snail
    ii Woodlouse/earthworm
  b iii Thrush/spider/hedgehog/ fox/sparrow hawk
  c Convert ammonia; into nitrates

Page 112 Microscopic life in water

1 a Advantage = no dehydration/little temperature change/water supports weight/easier to excrete waste; Disadvantage = difficult to maintain water balance/difficult to move against current
  b They are not competing for food
  c i Water will enter their cytoplasm; by osmosis
    ii Water is pumped into a vacuole; using energy; vacuole empties water to the outside
       (Any 2 = 1 mark each)
       (If drawing a diagram must include labels with same points as above.)
2 a Algae feed on the nutrients; algae population increases; algae start to die off; bacteria decompose algae using up oxygen; animals die from lack of oxygen
       (Any 3 = 1 mark each)
  b Small amounts pesticides are eaten by small organisms; larger animals feed on them/idea of a food chain; pesticides build up/are not broken down in larger animals; concentration increases enough to kill them; this is bioaccumulation   *(Any 3 = 1 mark each)*

Page 113 Enzymes in action

1 a

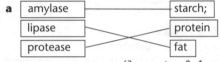

       (3 correct = 2; 1 or 2 correct = 1 mark)
  b i Makes a sweeter sugar
    ii Glucose; fructose   *(Any order)*
2 a Easier to separate enzyme from product; less purification needed; enzyme can be reused; continuous process so cheaper to run   *(Any 2 = 1 mark each)*
  b Lactase
  c i Cannot digest lactose
    ii Lactose not digested (by cat); bacteria ferment lactose; gas builds up; causes diarrhoea/wind
       (Any 2 = 1 mark each)

Page 114 Genetic engineering

1 a Transgenic
  b i Cut open the DNA of second organism; add the DNA from the first organism to that of the second one
    ii Restriction
  c Also add genes to make bacteria resistant to antibiotics; grow bacteria on (agar containing) antibiotic; if bacteria grow they are resistant
2 a Make crops resistant to weed killers; make crops produce other chemicals
  b Unsure if food is safe to eat; could damage the environment; other plants could become resistant to weed killers   *(Any 2 = 1 mark each)*
3 Gene for insulin is cut out of human DNA; gene is put into plasmid; plasmid placed into bacteria; bacteria are cloned
       (Any 3 = 1 mark each)